THE U.S. BISHOPS AND THEIR CRITICS

THE U.S. BISHOPS AND THEIR CRITICS

AN ECONOMIC AND ETHICAL PERSPECTIVE

WALTER BLOCK

THE FRASER
INSTITUTE

Canadian Cataloguing in Publication Data

Block, Walter, 1941-
The U.S. Bishops and their critics

A discussion of the document: Catholic social teaching and
the U.S. economy.
Bibliography: p.
ISBN 0-88975-085-8

1. Catholic Church. National Conference of Catholic
Bishops. Catholic social teaching and the U.S. economy.
2. Church and social problems – United States.   3. Church
and social problems – Catholic Church.   4. United States –
Economic Policy – 1981 –   I. Fraser Institute (Vancouver,
B.C.)   II. Title.

BX1795.E27B56 1986   261.8'5'0973   C86-091481-X

CONTENTS

Appendix/103

ABOUT THE AUTHOR

Walter Block is Senior Economist at the Fraser Institute and Director of its Centre for the Study of Economics and Religion. Born in Brooklyn, New York in 1941, Dr. Block received his B.A. from Brooklyn College in 1964 and his Ph.D. from Columbia University in 1972. He has taught Micro-economics, Industrial Organization, Urban Economics, and Political Economy at Stony Brook, State University of New York; the City College of New York, New York University; Baruch College, City University of New York; and Rutgers University, New Jersey; and has worked in various research capacities for the National Bureau of Economic Research, the Tax Foundation, and *Business Week* magazine.

Dr. Block has published numerous popular and scholarly articles on economics and is an economic commentator on national television and radio. He lectures widely on public policy issues to university students, service, professional and religious organizations. Dr. Block is Editor of the Fraser Institute books *Zoning: Its Costs and Relevance* (1980); *Rent Control: Myths and Realities* (1981); *Discrimination, Affirmative Action and Equal Opportunity* (1982); *Taxation: An International Perspective* (1984); *Morality of the Market: Religious and Economic Perspectives* (1985); *Reaction: The New Combines Investigation Act* (1986), and is the author of *Amending the Combines Investigation Act* (1982); *Focus: On Economics and the Canadian Bishops* (1983); and *Focus: On Employment Equity: A Critique of the Abella Royal Commission on Equality* (1985).

CHAPTER 1
INTRODUCTION*

The U.S. Catholic Bishops are to be congratulated for their initiative in entering the treacherous waters of economic and public policy analysis. Although the present response to their Pastoral Letter (henceforth called BP, for "Bishop's Pastoral") is highly critical in many regards, the publication of this document is still most gratefully received.

"Catholic Social Teaching and the U.S. Economy" comes to us in a historical context where government, despite some recent movement toward de-regulation, still takes upon itself an excessive role in economic affairs. Indeed, it is no exaggeration to say that the activity of the state dominates the economy. In such a situation, it is crucial that "mediating structures," institutions which lie between the citizen and government, be encouraged as much as possible. And the church is now, as it has always been, a mediating structure *par excellence*. BP is thus welcome if for no other reason than as a means of promoting an alternative to the voice of government in the determination of how society ought to be organized.

But the bishops' letter on economics has numerous merits of its own. Among the many virtues of this communication (discussed in detail in the Appendix to the present monograph) is the moral courage which underlies it, and the fact that this exercise in free speech — despite harsh criticisms to the effect that it should never have been written — safeguards the right to be heard of the espousers of other unpopular opinions. In addition, BP embodies a justified measure of moral indignation, its "preferential option

---

*The author would like to thank the following for helpful suggestions and comments, not all of whose advice he had the wisdom to incorporate: Kenneth Boulding, Kenneth Elzinga, Paul Heyne, James Johnston, Dianne Kennedy, Philip Lawler, Richard John Neuhaus, Michael Novak, Michael Parkin, Robert Rogowsky, James Sadowsky, James Schall, George Stigler, Michael Walker.

for the poor" focuses long overdue attention on the plight of this segment of the population, and it insightfully explores the role of the government in enriching the wealthy. As well, this missive analyses the naturalness of wealth, it quite properly deems as "immoral" the nation's falling but still significant rate of unemployment, and it courageously refuses to make concessions to the latter-day Malthusians who demand massive birth control measures as a means of curing world starvation.

PART ONE

PHILOSOPHY

CHAPTER 2

RIGHTS AND LIBERTIES

Having very briefly noted the praiseworthy elements of BP, we are now ready to consider the errors committed by the authors of this document. In what is to follow, we shall claim that the bishops have committed many and serious mistakes of commission and omission, of fact and value, of philosophy and economics. Lest there be any misinterpretation, however, let it now be said that none of these lapses from logic justify a demand that the bishops remain silent. Whose work, after all, is error free — on this side of the Garden of Eden?

I. POSITIVE ECONOMIC "RIGHTS"

Positive economic "rights" form one of the basic building blocks of the bishops' entire philosophy. The adherence to this position appears early in the BP. It is repeated on numerous occasions, it is the mainstay of Section II, Ethical Norms for Economic Life, and it informs much of their discussion in Part Two, which is devoted to public policy recommendations.
For example, the bishops demand that

> the nation must take up the task of framing a new national consensus that all persons have rights in the economic sphere and that society has a moral obligation to take the necessary steps to ensure that no one among us is hungry, homeless, unemployed, or otherwise denied what is necessary to live with dignity.[1]

And several of the bishops' supporters have carried this even one step further, explicitly calling for a new "Economic Bill of Rights," to supplement that which is already part of the U.S. Constitution.[2]

This concept, however, is deeply flawed, and even mischievous. In order to demonstrate this, we shall compare the traditional view of negative rights with the newer "variety" urged by the bishops. The disparity between them shall be a measure of just how different are the bishops' "positive rights" from those in the traditional view.

In classical philosophy, negative rights or negative liberty consist solely of the right not to have physical force, or the threat thereof, initiated against oneself. Each person, then, has the right not to be murdered, raped, robbed, assaulted, battered, etc. The doctrine of positive "rights," in contrast, typically holds that people have the right to food, clothing, shelter, and, depending on which variant is under discussion, to a reasonable lifestyle, to non-discriminatory behaviour, to meaningful relationships, to psychological well-being, to employment, to a decent wage, etc.

One basic problem with the so-called positive "rights" is that they are not really rights at all. Rather, they are aspects of wealth, or power, or control over the environment.

To illustrate the stark differences between the two very dissimilar concepts of rights, we contrast them in several dimensions.

Environmental dependency

Negative rights are independent of time, space, location and condition. They apply right now, but they were just as appropriate and pertinent 10,000 years ago. They are completely independent of circumstances. It was a rights violation for one caveman to club another over the head in prehistoric times, and this will hold true for spacemen 10,000 years in the future as well.

Positive "rights," in contrast, are highly environmentally dependent. If people have a positive "right" to food, there must be food available, otherwise they shall be deprived of their rights. And this may be impossible in certain eras, (during the seven "lean years" of the Bible), climes (the Arctic), locations (the Sahara). All that is needed for negative rights to be respected, in contrast, is that all people refrain from initiatory violence.

Good will

Only an act of will on the part of all people is necessary that negative rights be entrenched. If all the earth's population suddenly resolved never again to engage in the first use of force, all negative rights violations will at one fell swoop have come to an end.

But this does not obtain in the case of positive rights. We may all be of the best will in the world, and yet not succeed in delivering the goods and services required to satisfy all positive human "rights" for the entire population of the earth.

Alteration

Negative rights are unchanging. They have always been precisely the same as they are right now and will always remain so.

Positive "rights" are subject to change, depending upon the never stable definition of "decency" or "minimum standards." People began to have "rights" to indoor plumbing, varieties in food, refrigerators, television sets, etc., only after these items became available. They always had the right not to be aggressed against.

Agency

Only a human being can violate negative rights. He or she can do so by launching force against an innocent person.

Both humans and nature, however, can violate positive "rights." People can do so, of course, by refusing to give of themselves and their property that which is due to others according to this doctrine. But nature can continue to undermine positive "rights" as well. Storms, floods, frosts, avalanches, volcanoes, meteors, fires, and other acts of God — all of these can deprive people in the satisfaction of their positive "rights." None of these tragedies are even relevant to negative rights.

Game theory

Negative rights are reminiscent of a positive sum game, in that if one person suddenly attains an increase in his negative rights (fewer people for some reason aggress against him, or do so to a lesser degree) there need not necessarily be a diminution in the negative rights enjoyed by anyone else.[3] The economic analogue of the positive sum game is trade, where both parties to a commercial arrangement gain at least in the *ex ante* sense — otherwise they would not have agreed to participate.

In contrast, positive "rights" are evocative of the zero sum game. The paradigm case of the zero sum game is poker. Here, unless there is something very strange indeed going on, the winnings and losings of the various players must exactly cancel out one another. This is similar to positive "rights" for if one person's allotment of clothing or shelter, for example, is enhanced, then that of some other people is necessarily reduced by the same amount.[4]

Charity

Under a regime of positive "rights," it is not just difficult to give charity to the poor, it is logically impossible! Even if the donor intends that his offering be charitable, it cannot be so. For if this philosophy of BP is correct, the poor recipient has a *right* to (part of) the wealth of the rich person, and he, in turn, has an *obligation* to hand it over.

The relation between donor and recipient can thus no longer be one of giver and receiver of charity. The poor recipient now approaches the rich donor not as a requester, or a beggar, but as a bill collector settling a debt. If the rich man refuses to make the payment, the poor one need not plead with him, as for alms; now, armed with positive "rights," he can *demand* of the wealthy person that he make good on his "obligation."

In contrast, if negative rights and only negative rights are operational, then charity is logically legitimate — as common sense indicates it to be.

The bishops cannot have it both ways. They can purchase positive "rights," but only at the cost of charity. But if they opt for the latter, they can no longer ask for tithes, they must now present bills.

Occam's Razor

There are already in circulation several perfectly good phrases which convey what positive "rights" are meant to communicate: wealth, power, riches. Adding to the language this additional and complex terminology of positive "rights" only serves to confuse matters.[5] The scientific laws of parsimony known under the rubric "Occam's Razor" are sufficient to rule this out of court.

Incumbency

Who is responsible for carrying out the obligations imposed on people by the two alternative views under consideration? With negative rights, the answer is clear. Everyone must refrain from engaging in physical coercion. There are no exceptions, whatsoever.

With positive "rights," matters are far less clear. Upon whom it is incumbent that he share his wealth with the less fortunate? People in the same nation? In the same state? In the same city, county or borough?

We can answer that everyone is obligated to share with those who are less fortunate. But this is a truly radical idea, and would empower foreigners to present themselves at our shores and not just request a division of our wealth with them, but to demand it.

Degree

The degree to which these rights must be respected is yet another dimension upon which the two doctrines diverge widely.

In the case of real rights (i.e., negative rights — which is a redundancy) the degree of compliance required is absolute. One is forbidden to physically aggress[6] against other people even slightly. One cannot touch even "a hair on their heads."[7] But this has no implication for the distribution of income, since this is irrelevant to the concerns of negative rights.

What of the case of positive rights? How far must go the redistribution process? We are never vouchsafed an answer in BP. Hence, we can only speculate.

The only philosophically satisfactory answer to this question is that the process must continue until absolute income/wealth equality has been achieved.[8] If the reason for the process itself is inequality, then as long as any vestige of inequality yet remains, its continuation would still appear to be justified.[9]

Government

The implications for the scope of government of the two alternative rights philosophies are also very different. Novak's views on this question are definitive:

> The concept of economic rights undermines the American idea of the limited state. Civil and political rights prevent the state from blocking God-given, unalienable rights. But economic rights empower the state to take positive actions, including the establishment of definitions, conditions, and procedures which beneficiaries must meet, and the seizing of powers over the economy necessary to meet them. This logically takes the form (in China) of population controls; (in the USSR) of mandatory displacement of the unemployed to employment as the state. directs (in Siberia, e.g.); and (in Poland) of control over political life by control over all employment. Economic rights inevitably increase the power of the state.[10]

In contrast, the type of government compatible with negative rights is a very limited one. Indeed, the classical liberals saw the protection of (negative) liberties as the main and most important function of their "night watchman" state.

Punishment

Violators of (negative) rights are commonly punished by the imposition of fines, and for serious offences, by jail sentences or even the death penalty. There exists an entire literature[11] on the tailoring of punishments to fit the particular crime.

No such thing exists, to say the least, in the case of positive "rights" violations. Indeed, the whole idea is abhorrent. The idea of punishing people for not living up to these so-called obligations is repugnant (especially when it is unclear which specific rich individuals are responsible for giving sustenance to which particular poor people).[12] And yet the concoction of just such a theory is a necessary condition for making any sense out of the doctrine of positive "rights." This failure sheds doubt on the seriousness with which even its own proponents take their theory.

Rights conflicts

While on the subject of rights, there is one last matter to be cleared up. Two different rights can only conflict in the case of positive "rights." Here, one person's boundaries can extend well into those of another. And when there is an overlap of rights mappings, there is conflict — and one, the other, or both of the "rights" shall have to be abrogated.

In the case mentioned by the bishops (#229, 300), the "rights" of Third World countries to export their goods to the U.S. are incompatible with the "rights" of domestic workers (who produce these items at a higher cost) to keep their jobs. Both sets of positive "rights" cannot possibly be respected. This leads to the conclusion that one, the other, or both cannot be rights at all.

In contrast, there is no such possibility of conflict in the realm of negative rights. The right of A not to be aggressed against cannot conflict with the identical right of B.

Egalitarianism

Given the presumption of equality in the area of rights ("we all have equal rights before the law") positive rights lead ineluctably to egalitarianism. If we all have equal positive "rights," and positive rights are nothing but a synonym for wealth, then forced and exact income equality is justified.

Needless to say, no such presumption of egalitarianism applies to negative rights. To be sure, we all have an equal right not to be coerced, but since this has nothing to do with wealth, egalitarianism cannot be deduced from such a system.

Let us summarize. We have seen how very different are the two concepts of rights. They sharply differ in at least thirteen regards, mentioned above. There is of course no law against couching a demand for wealth distribution in rights language, but this does confuse matters. We can say if we wish that positive "rights" are rights, but it is incumbent on us to keep in mind that the two versions of rights are greatly at odds with one another, and that this usage can only spread confusion.

II. THE COMMON GOOD

Scattered throughout BP are references to the "common good."[13] This is a most unsatisfactory state of affairs, since nowhere is this phrase explicated in any meaningful manner.[14] Given this situation, the "common good" can mean whatever its user asserts. Use of the phrase, under these conditions, can only be considered misleading.

In #330 the bishops hold that "the value and dignity of each person is no mere philosophical or theological assertion, but a living conviction...." In this moving and powerful statement, they align themselves with the glorious tradition of individualism. But such sentiments are completely incompatible with all talk elsewhere in the BP of a "common good." For people — real, alive, individual people — are so very different in their perceptions of what is and is not good for them. It is hard to see how such a thing as the "common good" can be reconciled with the dignity and individuality of each and every human being.

III. NON-PRODUCTIVE ENTERPRISE

On numerous occasions BP warns against the evils of producing goods or services which are inappropriate, non productive or unneeded. If this were merely MBA-type counselling against the manufacture of Edsels in the future, one could accept it as sound business advice, but wonder at its appearance in a document of this sort.

However, it is no such thing. Rather, it appears to be another hobby horse of the bishops, reflective of their lack of comprehension of the operation of the free marketplace.

Consider this statement: "The redirection of capital into endeavors that do not enhance or may even reduce the production of needed goods and services is a violation of stewardship" (#119).

That is as it may be; but of far greater importance, such activity will tend to render the entrepreneur in question a loser in the competitive struggle. Any firm which misallocates capital in such manner will lose money and if it persists in its error, it will eventually go bankrupt.

"To err is human," but one of the greatest glories of the free enterprise system is that mistakes are automatically penalized. And severely so. The bishops, therefore, need not worry unduly about any such occurrence.

Gentrification

Another presumed misallocation that arouses the ire of the bishops is gentrification:

> Elderly people become homeless because they lack the resources to purchase the apartments they live in when the owner converts the building into a condominium in a neighborhood undergoing gentrification (#93).

But this concern, once again, is groundless. First of all, much condominium conversion is due to either the presence of rent controls, or to fear of their future imposition. Such controls short-circuit the rental market, in effect giving incentives for landlords to convert their units to ownership status, i.e., condominiums.[15]

Secondly, the major reason for homelessness in the U.S. has very little indeed to do with gentrification. On the contrary, it is because of changing policy regarding the incarceration of people in mental hospitals.[16]

Thirdly, gentrification is but a synonym for upgrading, repairing and improving the housing stock. The greater the supply of housing available (quantity or quality) the lower will be the rents (other things equal). Poor tenants thus have very little indeed to fear from this form of privatized urban renewal.[17]

Luxuries are another item which have felt the wrath of the bishops in their quest to rid the market of its supposed resource misallocations (#s 105, 311).

Michael Novak's brilliant response to this charge is worth repeating: "The (BP) faults investments in 'luxury consumer goods' ... (but) which 'luxury consumer goods' should be halted or diminished? By whose authority ...?"[18]

Advertising

The last pet peeve under this heading we shall consider is the bishops' ill-considered attack on the advertising industry — one of our most creative and productive: "... modern communications media ... have made it possible to manipulate appetites ... by generating false needs'' (#140).

This criticism comes with particular ill grace in view of all the advertising campaigns religious groups themselves have launched, and of all the unpaid advertising from which religious institutions have benefited ("In God We Trust'' on the coinage, and "One Nation, Under God ..." in the Pledge of Allegiance). The desire for a religious life is not one that people are likely born with. It has to be developed — and advertising is part of this process.

The defense of advertising begins with the understanding that, whether we like the particular message or not, it is part of our rights of free speech. It is buttressed by the realization that what constitutes a "false" or "superfluous" need is often a subjective matter. Nor have the bishops offered a criterion upon which such a determination could be made. And it is solidified by an appreciation that advertising oils the wheels of the economy; if the people cannot be apprised of products and services available to them — in an attractive and interesting way — commerce may not grind to a complete halt, but it will be heavily retarded, and with it the bishops' hopes for an ebullient economy with adequate employment opportunity.[19]

IV. PEOPLE BEFORE PROFITS

In BP the bishops succumb, unfortunately, to one of the hoariest of economic fallacies: that the market places profits before people (#106).[20]

Were this charge correct, profits could be attained literally by ignoring the wishes of customers. But a moment's reflection will show that the very opposite is true. Profits are earned by satisfying the paying customer, by anticipating his every wish, not by ignoring him. The firms which have shown healthy bottom lines — IBM, Toyota, Heinz, Coca Cola, McDonalds, — have done so by providing for millions of consumers precisely what they want. It is only government bureaucracies — public education, the post office, the motor vehicle bureau — which can afford to alienate the public. They, after all, were under no profit constraint which compelled them to gratify the customer.[21]

Notes

1. See 36, p. 338; see especially #s 174-89, but also #s 90-150, 258, 273. Wolfe has called this section the "real heart of the pastoral." See 39, p. 11. All paragraph (#) references are to document 36. All such numerical citations refer to the bibliography, pages 125-127.

2. See 5, pp. 129-30; see also 26, p. 32.

3. Tom Bethell incorrectly applies this insight to voting rights: "Extending the right (to vote) to more people (such as blacks, who were previously disenfranchised) would not take it away from the previously enfranchised. This same reason applies, obviously, to free speech, the freedom to worship, the right to bear arms, etc." (*The American Spectator*, July 1982, p. 14; material in brackets supplied by present author.) This argument does apply to free speech, worship, the right to bear arms and other negative liberties (the right to do anything one wishes — except to initiate force) but it does not apply to voting, which is a positive, not a negative right. We can see this when we realize that although the previously enfranchised can still vote, the effectiveness of their ballot has now become diluted. Nor is this a mere academic quibble with no real world implication — as the present South African crisis will attest.

4. Note that police protection, even though used primarily to enhance negative rights, is itself a resource, an aspect of wealth, and thus an instance of positive "rights." If one person has been accorded more police protection, another person must necessarily be given less.

5. Behind the use of positive "rights," of course, is the attempt to wrest from the concept of rights some of its lustre, and apply it to the otherwise far less savory policy of coercively transferring income from rich to poor.

6. For an analysis of how rights philosophy is applied to matters of ecology, environmentalism and external diseconomies, see Murray N. Rothbard, "Law, Property, Rights and Air Pollution," *Cato Journal*, Vol. 2, No. 1, Spring, 1982, pp. 55-99.

7. Why is only physical aggression proscribed? Why not psychological damage, or "mental cruelty" or some such? The short answer is that violations of law prohibiting physical coercion deserve jail sentences, while people who engage in psychological "evasiveness," or meanness, are typically guilty of no more than the exercise of their (negative) rights of free speech in ways to which someone objects. For an account of the dividing line between aggression and non-aggression, and for an explication of the national rights philosophy, see Robert Nozick, *Anarchy, State and Utopia*, New York: Basic Books, 1974, and Murray N. Rothbard, *The Ethics of Liberty*, Atlantic Highlands, N.J.: Humanities Press, 1982.

8. See Michael Levin, "Negative Liberty," *Social Philosophy and Policy*, 2:1, Autumn, 1984, pp. 84-100.

9. The logic of the view put forth in BP implies a "Brave New World" type of horror as well, given only the availability of the appropriate technology. For suppose there were machines which could transfer intelligence, or beauty, or serenity, or happiness, or even religious appreciation from one person to another. If those who are "rich" in these attributes really have an obligation to share with the less fortunate, they must be grabbed, kicking and screaming if need be, and forced to enter these personality-redistributing machines, no matter how personally shattering an experience it might be.

10. See 24, p. 9 (Novak uses the terms civil and political rights to refer to what we have been calling negative rights, and the phrase economic rights for our positive rights); H.L. Mencken's views on government are pithy and apropos: "The government consists of a gang of men exactly like you and me. They have, taking one with another, no special talent for the business of government, they have only a talent for getting and holding office. Their principal device to that end is to search out groups who pant and pine for something they can't get and to promise to give it to them. Nine times out of ten that promise is worth nothing. The tenth time it is made good by looting A to satisfy B. In other words, government is a broker in pillage and every election is sort of an advance auction sale of stolen goods."

11. *Assessing the Criminal: Restitution Retribution and the Legal Process*, Randy Barnett and John Hagel, eds., Cambridge, Mass." Ballinger, 1977; Murray Rothbard, *The Ethics of Liberty*, op. cit., pp. 85-95.

12. It will do no good to reply that government, through the tax and welfare system, should organize matters so that our positive "rights" obligations are met. For rights violations are an individual matter; specific, individual people should presumably be penalized if they fail to meet their responsibilities.

13. See #s 96, 119, 263, 269 and elsewhere. Nor is the Lay Letter free of this verbiage. See 25, pp. 23, 38, 59, for example.

14. In #96 the common good is "defined" as "the sum total of those conditions of social living, whereby human beings are enabled more fully and more readily to achieve their own perfection," but as can be appreciated, this is singularly unhelpful as a hint as to how to determine objectively what is and what is not in the common good.

15. *Rent Control: Myths and Reality*, Walter Block and Edgar Olson, eds., Vancouver: The Fraser Institute, 1981.

16. States Charles Krauthammer, 18, p. 51, "People are not sleeping in doorways because 'economic rights,' unlike political rights, do not hold a privileged position in the cultural and legal traditions of our nation. In fact, twenty-five years ago economic rights were, if anything, less enshrined than today, and there were no armies of grate-dwellers. There are today, largely as a result of one of the finest reformist impulses of the Kennedy years, the freeing of the mentally ill from the snakepits to which they had been consigned for a century.

It was decided to restore liberty to these people. But with liberty necessarily comes a diminution of security. We have an epidemic of homelessness today, not because we have yet to accept U.N. declarations on economic rights, but because of perennial conflict between liberty and security, a conflict most acutely manifest in those people most vulnerable to the ravages of freedom. We can do more for the homeless by forcing them into shelters. We might do still more by forcing them back into institutions." Inexplicably, the bishops appear to be actually *aware* of this reformist phenomenon discussed by Krauthammer. See #188.

17. However, they do indeed have much to fear from government-imposed urban renewal. (See Martin Anderson, *The Federal Bulldozer*, N.Y.: McGraw Hill, 1967.) It is unfortunate that the bishops aimed their arrows at gentrification when they could have far better served the principle of the preferential option for the poor by directing their critical attention at the Federal Urban Renewal Plan.

18. See 24, p. 13; 15, p. 11. It is said that "people who live in glass houses should not throw rocks." The bishops' opposition to luxuries is very dangerous, for there are people — especially on the other side of the Iron Curtain — who will conclude that religion is a luxury that cannot be afforded by the poor of the Third World.

19. For a fuller elucidation of these points, see F.A. von Hayek, "The Non-Sequitur of the 'Dependence Effect,'" in *Studies in Philosophy, Politics and Economics*, N.Y., Simon & Schuster, 1969, pp. 313-317; Israel Kirzner, *Competition and Entrepreneurship*, Chicago: The University of Chicago Press, 1973, pp. 135-186.

20. That this should not occur is singled out as "moral principle proclaimed by the church." See 39, p. 11. In contrast, the view of profit offered by the Lay Letter is nothing short of superlative. See 25, pp. 37-39.

21. The best short treatments of profits are Henry Hazlitt, *Economics in One Lesson*, N.Y.: Harper & Row, 1962, pp. 168-173; and Ludwig von Mises, "Profit and Loss" in *Planning for Freedom*, South Holland, Illinois: Libertarian Press, pp. 108-149.

PART TWO

ECONOMICS

CHAPTER 3

EMPLOYMENT

In Part Two of BP, the section devoted to policy applications, the bishops address themselves to four questions of economics: employment, poverty, economic democracy, and international relations. This commentary shall reply to each in the same order, in this and in the next three chapters.

I. UNIONS

It is not difficult to document the fact that BP champions unionism as commonly practiced in the United States as a means of promoting employment. Indeed, the sections of the report dealing with this "curious institution" are virtually nothing but[1] paeans of praise (#110-114, 181). In #148, the bishops go so far as to invite unions to organize their own church employees.[2] If anything, however, the Lay Letter is even more vociferous in its strident flattery of the U.S. union movement. As well, it exults in the fact that the Catholic Church had been a long-time and faithful supporter of organized labor,[3] a dubious distinction indeed.

The major reason given by the bishops for their unseemly support of American unionism is that "employers frequently possess greater bargaining power than do employees in the negotiation of wage agreements. Such unequal power may press workers into a choice between an inadequate wage and no wage at all" (#110).

But this rather seriously misconstrues the process of wage determination. In a free labor market, wages are basically set by the marginal revenue productivity[4] of the employee — not on the basis of bargaining power, scale of enterprises, or size of labor units. Were the bargaining power explanation for wage rates correct, remuneration would be negatively correlated with the concentration ratio; that is, industries with fewer employers would pay lower wages than ones with many — and pay would be unrelated to measures of productivity such as educational attainment. Needless to say, no evidence for this contention exists.

The Lay Letter, too, articulates its "full support for the principle of free and voluntary association in labor unions."[5]

But this is disingenuous. It is not even a rough approximation of how organized labor has and still continues to operate in the U.S.

Coercion

There are two kinds of unions possible — those which do all that they can to raise their members' wages and working conditions — except violate the (negative) rights of other people by initiating violence against them. These can be called "voluntary unions." And then there are those which do all they can to promote their members' welfare up to and including the use of physical brutality aimed at non-aggressing individuals.

With regard to the activity of "coercive unions" defined in this manner, Ludwig von Mises has stated:

> In all countries the labor unions have actually acquired the privilege of violent action. The governments have abandoned in their favor the essential attribute of government, the exclusive power and right to resort to violent coercion and compulsion. Of course, the laws which make it a criminal offense for any citizen to resort — except in case of self-defense — to violent action have not been formally repealed or amended. However, actual labor union violence is tolerated within broad limits. The labor unions are practically free to prevent by force anybody from defying their orders concerning wage rates and other labor conditions. They are free to inflict with impunity bodily evils upon strike-breakers and upon entrepreneurs and mandataries of entrepreneurs who employ strikebreakers. They are free to destroy property of such employers and even to injure customers patronizing their shops. The authorities, with the approval of public opinion, condone such acts. The police do not stop such offenders, the state attorneys do not arraign them, and no opportunity is offered to the penal courts to pass judgment on their actions. In excessive cases, if the deeds of violence go too far, some lame and timid attempts at repression and prevention are ventured. But as a rule they fail. Their failure is sometimes due to bureaucratic inefficiency or to the insufficiency of the means at the disposal of the authorities, but more often to the unwillingness of the whole governmental apparatus to interfere successfully.
>
> What is euphemistically called collective bargaining by union leaders and 'pro-labor' legislation is of a quite different character. It is bargain-

ing at the point of a gun. It is bargaining between an armed party, ready to use its weapons, and an unarmed party under duress. It is not a market transaction. It is a dictate forced upon the employer. And its effects do not differ from those of a government decree for the enforcement of which the police power and the penal courts are used. It produces institutional unemployment.

The treatment of the problems involved by public opinion and the vast number of pseudo-economic writings is utterly misleading. The issue is not the right to form associations. It is whether or not any association of private citizens should be granted the privilege of resorting with impunity to violent action. It is the same problem that relates to the activities of the Ku Klux Klan.

Neither is it correct to look upon the matter from the point of view of a 'right to strike.' The problem is not the right to strike, but the right — by intimidation or violence — to force other people to strike, and the further right to prevent anybody from working in a shop in which a union has called a strike. When the unions invoke the right to strike in justification of such intimidation and deeds of violence, they are on no better ground than a religious group would be in invoking the right of freedom of conscience as a justification of persecuting dissenters.

When in the past the laws of some countries denied to employees the right to form unions, they were guided by the idea that such unions have no objective other than to resort to violent action and intimidation. When the authorities in the past sometimes directed their armed forces to protect the employers, their mandataries, and their property against the onslaught of strikers, they were not guilty of acts hostile to 'labor.' They simply did what every government considers its main duty. They tried to preserve their exclusive right to resort to violent action.[6]

And in the view of Friedrich Hayek:

It cannot be stressed enough that the coercion which unions have been permitted to exercise contrary to all principles of freedom under the law is primarily the coercion of fellow workers. Whatever true coercive power unions may be able to wield over employers is a consequence of this primary power of coercing other workers; the coercion of employers would lose most of its objectionable character if unions were deprived of this power to exact unwilling support. Neither the right of voluntary agreement between workers not even their right to withhold their services in concert is in question.[7]

Who are the innocent persons against whom coercive union violence in the U.S. (and other countries) is directed? These are the people at the bottom of the employment ladder, the least, last, and lost of us, the individuals after whose welfare the bishops ask us to take particular concern in their principle of the preferential option for the poor. They are, in a word, the "scabs."

Scabs

Now scabs have had a very bad press. Even the appellation ascribed to them is one of derogation. But when all the loose and inaccurate verbiage is stripped away, the scab is no more than a poor person, oft-times unskilled, uneducated, under — or unemployed, perhaps a member of a minority group, who seeks nothing more than to compete in the labor market,[8] and there to offer his services to the highest bidder.

In fact, it is no exaggeration to consider the scab the economic equivalent of the leper. And we all know the treatment with regard to lepers urged upon us by ecclesiastical and biblical authorities.[9]

In their excessively pro (coercive) union stance, both the authors of BP and of the Lay Letter expose themselves as untrue to the morally axiomatic principle of the preferential option of the poor. The "poor," in this case, are not the princes of labor, organized into gigantic, powerful and coercive unions. Rather, they are the despised, downtrodden and denigrated scabs. If not, and if "poor" in this case is interpreted so as to refer to the coercively unionized workers, not to the scabs, then the principle of the preferential option for the poor falls into disrepute.

Needless to say, nothing said here mitigates against the legitimacy of voluntary unions, those which restrict themselves to mass walkouts and other non-invasive activity. The only difficulty is that at present, in modern day America, such entities are exceedingly scarce.

II. WAGES

Next, we consider the muddied waters of wage theory into which the bishops have launched themselves. On several occasions, scattered throughout the BP, they put themselves on record as calling for "just wages," or "adequate remuneration" (#377,110).[10]

One of the greatest intellectual tragedies of the church, one from which religious institutions are only now beginning to recover, is the medieval debate concerning the "just price." Evocative of questions such as "how many angels can dance on the head of a pin?'' the ''just price'' controversy is well on the way toward being resolved. And the answer? The just price for an item is whatever payment to which any pair of buyers and sellers can agree.

But now that the ''just price'' wars have been happily consigned to the dust bin of history, a fate they so richly deserve, along comes another equally trivial contention to again threaten the intellectual probity of ecclesiastical organizations, this one over ''just wages.'' Hopefully, this will soon go the way of the other, and we shall be left with the similar result that the just wage is any level of remuneration mutually acceptable to an employer and employee.

But such a solution, unfortunately, will have to overcome the best efforts of the bishops to the contrary. For in their view, ''Labor is not simply a commodity traded on the open market nor is a just wage determined simply by the level the market will sustain'' (#110).

This will not do, however. To be sure, labor is not simply a commodity like any other. For one thing, it cannot legally be traded, only rented. But the question is, What reason do the bishops put forth to justify their contention that a just wage is not that reached on the open market? And the answer is, none. They only concern themselves with the epistemological status of labor, but this is a red herring. Given that labor is not a commodity like others, we still have no case against considering the market wage the just one.

Another problem is that the bishops fail to state precisely what the just wage is. (They only assert what it is not, namely the market wage, i.e., the one agreed upon by two consenting parties). Yet it is obligatory on the person putting forth a claim to elucidate what it is, not what it is not.

Let us, in any case, make good on this oversight. To wit, we hereby assert, for the sake of argument, that the just wage is always and ever 120 percent of the market wage. That is, all workers are presently being exploited to the tune of 20 percent of their wages. Nor let us cavil at the arbitrariness of any such proposal. Instead, consider this far more fundamental objection to any specification of the just wage (apart from the market wage, whatever it is).

Suppose that someone willingly, happily and voluntarily wants to work for less than the ''just wage,'' whether determined in this way or in any other. Suppose, that is, that a church employee wants in effect to make a contribution to his employer in the form of a salary cut. Plaintively asks one writer ''whether the dedication of Christians who work for less than a 'just wage' is now to be deemed immoral? That would be a not-so-delicate break from the Christian history of radical vocation.''[11] It would also be equivalent to the claim that charity is immoral — when given by the worker to his boss in the form of a voluntary decrease in pay.

III. UNEMPLOYMENT

The crux of the bishops' position on unemployment can be found in #s 168-170, where they discuss its causes and cures. They begin with the victims of unemployment: the new entrants to the labor force such as teenagers, women and immigrants, people who have a greater tendency to change jobs, and to take longer in searching for new employment, because of relative unfamiliarity with labor markets. These demographic changes could thus very well elevate the amount of voluntary unemployment in a society, but this is outside of our concern.

Next to be considered as causes of unemployment are malinvestments, inability to cope with OPEC-inspired oil price increases, poor education and training, discrimination, competition from imports, small farm bankruptcies, and location in depressed city areas. Let us consider each in turn.

In malinvestments, the bishops have touched upon a crucial element in the Austrian school's theory of unemployment.[12] Indeed, it does little violence to the bishops' views to characterize them as a malinvestment theory of the business cycle. Unfortunately for the bishops' overall mission of promoting dirigisme, this is a theory of how government intervention into financial markets leads to depressions. Private malinvestments are self-limiting, as those responsible for the errors tend to lose the wherewithal with which to spike the economy.

The oil shocks of the 1970s certainly led to unemployment. The changes in energy prices encouraged some firms and industries, and discouraged others. Temporary or frictional unemployment was the inevitable result of the process of adjustment, where workers left the declining businesses and joined the expanding ones. But again the bishops can find little solace in their quest to statize the economy in this phenomenon. For it was government activity, particularly the price controls on oil which exacerbated the problem and directly caused the shortages and lineups for gas.[13]

Discrimination

The best empirical work indicates that discrimination is highly overblown as a cause of economic debility in general and of unemployment in particular. Other phenomenona — such as age, education, location, culture, marital status — appear to more accurately account for perceived racial, ethnic and gender differences. In any case, discrimination, to the very slight degree it has any measurable effect at all, would appear to impact wage levels, not unemployment.[14]

Competition from imports can certainly create temporary unemployment, and joblessness in particular sectors (textiles, autos, appliances, etc.). But it also creates opportunities to produce goods and services sought by the foreigners in trade for their exports to the domestic economy. This is not the place to elucidate the case for full free trade; we must content ourselves with merely claiming that a complete elimination of all international trade barriers would enhance world prosperity, and would not aggravate unemployment.[15] In any case, the bishops, happily, appear committed to free trade, at least with regard to the economically backward nations of the world (see below), so this "cause" of unemployment yields no dispute over public policy implications.

A complete analysis of the bishops' views on agricultural policy cannot be made at present. Instead, we shall limit ourselves to denying that small farm bankruptcies, in conjunction with the expansion of large "agribusiness" can yield additional unemployment. To the extent that this occurs, employees will merely shift over from the former to the latter. True, there will be some additional temporary unemployment from this source, but this is the result of any change, for better or for worse, as long as perfect knowledge of new job opportunities is unavailable.

Family farm

But suppose that agribusiness is, horrors!, more capital intensive than the small family farms it supplants. Will this not increase unemployment? No. It is only through greater efficiency that the large-scale farms — in a free market — can supplant the smaller ones. But greater efficiency, through the competitive process, leads to lower prices. Cheaper food will of course be a boon to all consumers. They can still buy as much as before, and now have money left over — money with which to purchase goods whose production will necessitate the hiring of the farm workers who were supplanted by the presumably more capital intensive larger farms. This is precisely what occurred when the capital-intensive "horseless" carriage of Henry Ford obliterated the family-oriented horse and buggy industry.

The bishops mention central area location in several major U.S. cities as a cause of economic disarray. This is indeed a puzzle. For cheek-by-jowl with these depressed areas are some of the most vibrant economies in the world. Unfortunately, space limitations prohibit the full attention this complex topic deserves. But a brief answer would point to cultural dislocation and family breakdown due to rampant welfare dependency, to mischievous government policies in housing (rent control, public housing, urban renewal, zoning), and to the failure of government to control crime.[16]

Last on the list of causes of unemployment considered by BP is the fight against inflation. This bit of nonsense was perpetrated on a gullible public by the Keynesian school of thought, and the bishops give it the backs of their collective hand — a fate it richly deserves.[17] According to this theory, there was supposed to be a trade-off between inflation and unemployment. But when both phenomena took place at the same time in the 1970s — something not contemplated in Keynesian theory — this spelled the death knell of that perspective.

That is it! There simply is no more. These three brief paragraphs (#s 168-170) exhaust all the causes of unemployment mentioned by the bishops in an effort several years in the making. It doesn't take a professional economist to see that the bishops and their minions failed to come fully to grips with the real causes of unemployment.

Pricing out of market

Unfortunately, the major cause of unemployment is not addressed in the BP. Legislation that artificially boosts wages above the productivity levels of workers to whom they apply is the missing factor in the bishops' analysis. Examples of this phenomenon include the minimum wage law, labor codes which enable unions to "bargain" to this end, and enactments such as Davis-Bacon which also lift wages above free market levels.[18]

It is highly disconcerting that in the bishops' analysis of the causes of unemployment, they never even consider government legislation of this sort as the possible culprit. Nor is it as if they had never heard of the instances of this phenomenon, for example, the minimum wage law. This is specifically mentioned in #210 — but not, unfortunately — in the context of unemployment creation.

This omission is particularly disappointing in view of the statement in the BP: "Among black teenagers aged 16 to 19 who are seeking jobs unemployment reaches the tragic figure of 41.7 percent, while for blacks aged 20 to 24 it is a discouraging 26.3 percent" (#162). The bishops are quite correct to be concerned with this state of affairs, since unemployed young blacks certainly qualify for coverage under the principle of the preferential option for the poor. But minimum wage legislation strikes particularly at youthful blacks.

In reply to a question whether some groups are hurt more by the minimum wage than others, Milton Friedman stated:

Yes, indeed. Take Negro teenagers, for example. We all know the terrible social problems being caused, especially in our large cities, by the high rate of unemployment among Negro teenagers. The fact is — it can be demonstrated statistically — the minimum wage rate is a major cause of Negro teenage unemployment. Of all the laws on the statute books of this country, I believe the minimum wage law probably does the Negroes the most harm. It is not intended to be an anti-Negro law but, in fact, it is.[19]

This finding has been reached in literally hundreds, if not thousands, of scholarly books, articles, and Ph.D. theses.[20] Indeed, it is hardly an exaggeration to say that of all economic propositions, the one which states that "A minimum wage increases unemployment among young and unskilled workers" is among those that would receive the most assent from economists.[21]

Inflated wage levels

It is thus greatly to be regretted that the bishops did not see fit to mention governmental policies which artificially force up wages in connection with the creation of unemployment. This omission is so serious it casts doubt on the value of much of their work on this subject.

Having failed to uncover the major causes of unemployment, the bishops' discussion of its cures can only be further disappointing. They begin by telling us that "as a nation the U.S. has had considerable experience in trying to generate jobs and reduce unemployment. From 1932 through 1943 the U.S. government undertook a range of work-relief and public works programs that still hold some lessons for the present" (#171; see also #180). Based on this, they advocate such modern equivalents as CETA, Youth Corps, and other similarly discredited initiatives. But this really will not pass muster. Says Ludwig von Mises, as if in anticipation of this very proposal:

> If government spending for public works is financed by taxing the citizens or borrowing from them, the citizens' power to spend and invest is curtailed to the same extent as that of the public treasury expands. No additional jobs are created.[22]

And if they try to finance these work-relief programs by printing up additional dollar bills, they will only succeed in creating inflation, which will misallocate resources, penalize those on fixed incomes (the widows and orphans), destabilize the economy and thus create further unemployment.

BP cautions against "leaf raking" and "make work" jobs which produce items for which there is no demand (#174). And well it might. But the bishops fail to grapple with the fact that this is precisely the typical result of public sector job creation efforts. And the reason is simple. Any private enterprises which hire people to manufacture products not in demand soon go broke, and misallocate resources no further. It is only in government that decisions of this sort are immune to profit and loss incentives and other such market forces.

Job training

Another recommendation is for stepped-up apprenticeship and job-training programs (#181).

The problem with retraining, however, is that it takes time, usually a year or two; for the more complex skills, it can take even three or four or more. The needs of industry, moreover, have an infuriating way of changing — and changing drastically — between the time of initial enrollment and graduation. In other words, there is a serious forecasting problem. And this is not just a matter of forecasting the levels of future economic activity — a task that is daunting on its own. As well, someone has to make a stab at anticipating whether the next generation of workers will be required to produce widgets or gizmos!

But government is not without a response to this challenge. In order to mesh training with future skills' demands, the federals are continually working on a formula for long range forecasting of such changes.

Accurate forecasting, however, is easier to assume than to accomplish. The government's record in this regard is far from impressive — not to put too fine a point on it. Numerous graduates of such courses in the past are unable to find employment. And the most reasonable prognostication is that many of the high-tech jobs the government is currently undertaking for its unfortunate client-victims are almost obsolete.

Clearly, the answer is to eliminate the heavy hand of government, root and branch, from this most crucial of endeavors. Instead, we would do well to rely upon the far better record of private enterprise in this regard.

In the marketplace, a school that retrained graduates for jobs no longer in existence would soon enough go the way of the Edsel. Only those which successfully predict the future course of industrial events can grow and prosper.

But this safety net, or safety valve, is unavailable to public sector enterprise. Who ever heard of a governmental effort allowed to go bankrupt because of innumerable failures?

That is why the sooner the funds being frittered away on public sector retraining are returned to the private marketplace, the better will be the prospects for the unemployed.

Plant closings

The bishops also inveigh against "plant closings" (#183). They advocate that firms be prohibited from "simply casting aside" employees, and would force them to pay for retraining programs. But their suggestions are a recipe for economic disaster. If plants are prohibited from closing, or if such roadblocks as advocated by the bishops are placed in their way, then new plants are less likely to open in the first place. Rather, investors will risk their funds in areas more hospitable to capital.[23]

How do the critics of BP compare to that document the question of unemployment? There is some improvement, but not much.[24] The Lay Letter, for example, is too biased in favor of coercive unionism to even contemplate the role played by this institution in forcing wages above productivity levels. Nor does it oppose organized labor-supported minimum wage legislation.[25] Its authors ignore the fact that the labor movement has devastated the lives of millions of young people in this manner. Rather, it contents itself with pointing out the important role of small business and entrepreneurship in creating "some 26 million ... new jobs ... between 1970 and early 1984."[26]

And Novak

> suggests that Catholic laypersons in suburban parishes, skilled in entrepreneurship, should be invited to put personal efforts into helping Catholics in poor parishes to teach such skills and help local economic activists get businesses started. In poor neighbourhoods, there is invariably a lot of work to be done and a lot of unemployed labor — some catalyst is needed to put these two factors together creatively.[27]

Now this is all well and good. Certainly, no one can oppose entrepreneurship. And who can be against voluntary efforts embodying mutual aid? But such advice leaves open a gaping hole: Why is it, for goodness sake, that the market has not acted as a catalyst in this manner?

A vacuum

On the face of it, this is indeed puzzling. For "a lot of work to be done" in close proximity to "a lot of unemployed labor" adds up to a vast opportunity to earn profits. And just as nature abhors a vacuum, the market abhors an unseized profit opportunity. How is it that no entrepreneur has already rushed in "to put these two factors together creatively?"

The reason is, of course, that government has put up a whole host of roadblocks, foremost among them, as we have seen, the minimum wage law. Yes, to be sure, some few Catholic laypersons may well take up the invitation of the Lay Letter, and some good may be done in the economically deprived areas of our large cities as a result. But their motivation will be charitable, and benevolent, not commercial. That is why it will never amount to more than a drop in the bucket. It will not be until thousands of entrepreneurs have a profit-oriented incentive to hire young black males that any appreciable dent will be made in their tragic unemployment rate. And this cannot occur until that vicious, depraved and immoral piece of legislation, the minimum wage law, is repealed, and salt sown where once it lay.

In closing its eyes to the real source of unemployment for teenagers, for the unskilled, for the uneducated, and in fastening its attention on peripheral issues, the Lay Letter does little service toward an eradication of this problem and renders its own advice highly problematic.

IV. WORKING CONDITIONS

For the economist, the distinction between wages and working conditions is at best a superficial one. Both are merely different forms of compensation, and market forces will ensure that workers are paid these two parts of their salaries roughly in the desired proportions.[28]

Nevertheless, it behooves us to consider indirect salary payments in some detail, as there is some concern with it in the BP and in the literature surrounding it.

For example, the bishops claim that the economy ought to be organized so as to "enable persons to find a significant measure of self-realization in their labor" (#77).[29] What does this mean? Presumably, that workers should take a higher proportion of their salaries in the form of a specific type of improved working conditions: fewer assembly lines which create "anomie," perhaps a slower pace of work, more on-the-job creativity, less repetitiveness, etc.

It is folly to assume that it would be costless to radically restructure U.S. industry in order to cater to the presumed delicate sensibilities of employees for self-expression, self-realization, and other desiderata of "humanist" psychology. And the costs of these rearrangements, this consumption-on-the-job so to speak, would have to be borne by the workers, those in whose behalf the bishops are presumably demanding the requisite restructuring. Nowhere in the BP, however, is any reason given for asking workers to take a cut in take-home pay that these changes would necessitate.

It would be a waste, moreover, to undertake any such alteration in American industry. For one thing, as we have seen, there is no reason to believe that entrepreneurs are not now delivering the total wage bill in at least roughly the form most desired by their employees. For another, the option desired by the bishops for the working population is now open to it in a more direct manner.

A choice

There is always a choice between two kinds of jobs. On the one hand there is relatively high paying employment in mines, mills, farms, and factories, where people are not "respected as persons," where the tasks are "degrading," "exploitative" and even filthy, where their individuality is not catered to, and where they are treated, in short, as "instruments of production." On the other hand there are careers in pottery making (on an individual, not a mass basis), basket weaving, sculpture, tapestry, knitting, stained glass and other such arts and crafts. These don't pay much, but they certainly enhance the artistic sensibilities of the people involved. They can work at their own pace, when the artistic mood strikes them; they have no boss breathing down their neck, and they never have to punch a time clock. A correction. It is not true that these jobs are low paying. The direct financial remuneration may be sparse, but the indirect compensation is very high indeed — in the form of pleasant working conditions, scope for individual creativity, etc.

What are we to say of people who prefer the former type of employment (high direct pay coupled with "poor" working conditions)? That they are immoral, unGodly and irreligious? Not a bit of it. Only that they prefer to take their consumption pleasures off the job, not on the job, as do their arts and crafts oriented colleagues.

The authors of BP and Lay Letter have gone so far wrong in their analysis because of a profound misunderstanding of the economic category of work. Work is defined, for the economist, as that which has no intrinsic or even superficial interest or value. Work is that which the person in question would prefer *not* to do. Indeed, the only (voluntary) way to get people to work is to compensate them for its onerousness — by paying them. If a person likes his job, he is not at work, but rather at play, for play is defined as that which the relevant person would be willing to do without compensation.[30] "The play is compensation enough" is how this might be described.

Pay for play

Many thousands of people in the U.S. economy, the greatest the world has ever seen all throughout recorded history, are fortunate enough to be paid a salary to "play." That is to say, they have jobs of the sort that they would be delighted to do for free, provided only that they had sufficient funds to maintain their chosen life style[31] and that their jobs, for some reason, no longer paid salaries.

Many additional thousands of people have jobs at which they "play" for some weeks of the year, or days of the week, or hours of the day; only at other times is their employment onerous, and hence "work."

The positive element of the bishops' concern for improved working conditions translates into a wish that one day all people on this earth may earn their living through "play." That is as it should be in the ideal society, and if governments would cease and desist from their economic interferences, that day would come that much sooner.

But there are two distinctly negative aspects of this present call for "co-creation." First, it is a piece of paternalism. The bishops do not know what is in the best economic interests of the American worker, even though they are not unforthcoming in telling him about it. People show no evidence of wanting lower pay in return for being treated like temperamental artisans. Secondly, were these policies ever implemented (this is exceedingly unlikely, but stranger things have occurred) it would severely damage the U.S. economy. It's great engines of production would have to be all but dismantled, as the managerial techniques made famous in the movie "9 to 5" were imposed. Mass production, assembly lines, and other such techniques may not be aesthetically pleasing to ecclesiastics, but they enable the working class to enjoy a far greater standard of living than could be afforded by more effete methods of production.

Notes

1. However, there is one slight rebuke given by BP to organized labor. In #135 American unionism is upbraided for supporting protectionism.

2. But have they anticipated the likelihood that this might encourage the actual picketing of church services? For an instance of this behaviour, see editorial entitled, "And on the Seventh Day, God was Picketed," *North Shore News*, April 5, 1981, p. 1.

3. See 25, pp. 35-37; this point is also made in 17, p. 26. Novak, moreover, had the intestinal fortitude to publicize the fact that "Lane Kirkland kindly telephoned to thank us for our strong support of labor unions, and Monsignor George Higgins ('the labor priest') of the bishops' staff, to his credit, wrote a column lauding our treatment of unions as one of the best of its sort he had seen in his lifetime." See 22, p. 20.

4. This is not the place to expound on the process by which wages are set. An exegesis of this phenomenon may be found in practically any college economic textbook. The interested reader may consult J.R. Hicks, *The Theory of Wages*, New York: St. Martins Press, 1963, Second Edition, especially chapter 1, pp. 1-22, entitled, "Marginal Productivity and the Demand for Labor;" C.E. Ferguson, *Microeconomic Theory*, Homewood, Illinois: Richard D. Irwin, 1972, pp. 393-425; George Stigler, *The Theory of Price*, New York: MacMillan, 1962, especially chapter 11, pp. 187-203, entitled, "The pricing of productive services;" Alfred Stonier and Douglass C. Hague, *A Textbook of Economic Theory*, New York: John Wiley, 1964, especially chapter XI, entitled, "Marginal Productivity."

5. See 25, p. 36.

6. Ludwig von Mises, *Human Action, op. cit.*, pp. 777-79.

7. F.A. von Hayek, *The Constitution of Liberty*, Chicago: Regnery, Gateway, ed., 1960, p. 269. See also Sylvester Petro, *The Labor Policy of the Free Society*, New York, Ronald Press, 1957; Roscoe Pound, *Legal Immunities of Labor Unions*, Washington, D.C.: American Enterprise Association, 1957. Says Morgan O. Reynolds in *Power and Privilege: Labor Unions in America*, New York: Manhattan Institute for Policy Research, 1984, p. 50: "Hitting a person over the head with a baseball bat is much less likely to be treated as criminal if the person wielding the bat is an organized (i.e. unionized) worker in a labor dispute." See also Peter Bauer and John Burton, *Focus: On the Power of Britain's Organized Labour: Sources and Implications*, Vancouver: The Fraser Institute, 1983, especially chapter I entitled, "The Overmighty Subjects."

8. It is sometimes alleged that the union is justified in visiting violence upon the scab, since it is he who initiates coercion by daring to "steal" the job "owned" by the organized worker in the first place. But this claim cannot stand analysis. The employed worker no more owns "his" job than does the outsider. An employment contract is nothing but an agreement between two willing parties. Neither one of them can own it. In a free society, a society of contract, not of status, each person is free to enter the labor market and compete with all others. The unionized, employed worker is no more justified in utilizing violence to restrict the entry into the job market of the scab than would be the scab in employing initiatory force against the organized laborer.

9. This point was made in Walter Block, "Liberation Theology," *Grail: An Ecumenical Journal*, Vol. 1, No. 3, September 1985, pp. 75-85. See also Walter Block, *Defending the Undefendable*, N.Y.: Fleet Press, 1976, chapter entitled, "The Scab," pp. 237-41.

10. Also see 8, p. 107; 36, p. 339.

11. See 29, p. B8. Our just-wage-as-market-wage hypothesis, it will be appreciated, is immune from this objection. For the market wage is whatever level of pay the person who seeks a salary cut finally settles upon. Thus, even in this case, the market and the "just" wage must always be equal.

12. See F.A. Hayek, *Prices and Production*, London: Routledge, 1932; idem., *Monetary Theory and the Trade Cycle*, New York: Kelley, 1966; *idem.*, *Profits, Interest and Investment*, New York, Kelley, 1975; *idem.*, *The Pure Theory of Capital*, Chicago: University of Chicago Press, 1975; Ludwig von Mises, *The Theory of Money and Credit*, New York: Foundation for Economic Education, 1971; Murray N. Rothbard, *America's Great Depression*, Kansas City: Sheed & Ward, 1972.

13. Hendrik S. Houthakker, "No Use for Controls," Barrons, November 8, 1971, pp. 7-8.

14. See *Discrimination, Affirmative Action and Equal Opportunity*, W. Block and M. Walker, eds., Vancouver: The Fraser Institute, 1982, especially the contributions of Gary Becker, Thomas Sowell, and Walter Williams. See also 19, p. 114, and Walter Block and Michael Walker, *Focus: On Employment Equity: A Critique of the Abella Royal Commission Report on Equality in Employment*, Vancouver: The Fraser Institute, 1985.

15. See Milton Friedman, *Capitalism and Freedom*, Chicago: University of Chicago Press, 1967, pp. 56-74.

16. See Edward C. Banfield, *The Unheavenly City Revisited*, Boston: Little, Brown, 1974; Jane Jacobs, *The Death and Life of Great American Cities*, New York: Random House, 1961; Charles Murray, *Losing Ground: American Social Policy 1950-1980*, New York: Basic Books, 1985.

17. On the question of inflation and monetary policy, see Milton Friedman and Anna Schwartz, *A Monetary History of the United States 1867-1960*, New Jersey: Princeton University Press, 1963; Ludwig von Mises, *The Theory of Money and Credit*, New York: Foundation for Economic Education, 1971.

18. See Walter Williams, *The State Against Blacks, op. cit.*

19. Yale Brozen and Milton Friedman, *The Minimum Wage Rate: Who Really Pays?*, Washington, D.C.: The Free Society Association, 1966, pp. 10-11.

20. For a brief but representative sample bibliography see *Focus: On the Canadian Bishops, op. cit.*, p. 66, also pp. 45-55.

21. This precise question was put to a sample of 211 U.S. economists; 87.7 percent either "generally agreed" or "agreed with provisions." See Bruno S. Frey, Werner W. Pommerehne, Friedrich Schneider, and Guy Gilbert, "Consensus and Dissension Among Economists: An Empirical Inquiry," *American Economic Review*, Vol. 74, No. 5, December 1984, pp. 986-94.

22. *Human Action, op. cit.*, p. 776.

23. For a masterful and insightful evisceration of the idea of legally prohibiting or discouraging plant closings as a means of promoting economic well-being, see Richard McKenzie, "The Case for Plant Closures," *Policy Review*, Winter 1981), pp. 119-134.

24. There is one absolutely magnificent statement in this literature, however, which is so brilliant and scintillating it deserves to be engraved in the minds of all who in future ever partake in discussions of youthful unemployment. States the Lay Letter, "Ray Kroc, who in his later years invented the concepts on which McDonald's is based, gave more employment to teenaged youths than all the programs of the federal government put together, costing the government not a penny and paying taxes for the privilege." See 25, p. 41.

25. There should be no doubt that this is a coercive piece of legislation: it incarcerates or fines employers whose only "crime" is to offer to pay employees at below minimum level wages.

26. See 25, p. 66.

27. See 26, p. 31.

28. Suppose that workers desired to be paid in the proportion 80 percent for money wages and 20 percent for working conditions (safety, comfort, air conditioning, variety, interest, challenge, scope for "self-realization," clothing allowances, location, convenience, etc.) and that employers have somehow got this wrong and now offer only 75 percent (as much as 85 percent) of the total salary in direct compensation and 25 percent (only 15 percent) in the form of indirect compensation for improved working conditions. It is easy to see that any entrepreneur who sees this could earn additional profits. All he need do is offer the right proportion (80 percent-20 percent). Then, he could have better choice of workers, leading to more profits, since his quit rates would be lower than those of his competitors (other things equal). Alternatively, he could offer the correct 80 percent-20 percent proportion, but reduce the total wage paid; i.e. he could decrease the total of money wages plus non-money wages, to, say 99 percent of its former level. If he could still attract a sufficient staff, his profit would come from paying more efficient workers a lower total salary (but in more appropriate proportions) than commonly earned elsewhere. Quite likely the movement toward correct proportionality would work in both these ways.

29. This call is echoed in 39, p.11; and according to the Lay Letter, 25, p. 26, "Every human being who works must be respected as a person. None is merely 'an instrument of production.'"

And *Business Week*, 8, p.110, cites the Reverend David Hollenback, a Jesuit theologian, and consultant on the bishops' drafting committee, to the effect that "work is theologically important: Catholic teaching sees human work as co-creation, a sharing in the continuing work of God, the Creator. Work that is degrading or exploitative is man's sinful distortion of God's purpose."

30. Says Murray Rothbard in this regard, (*Man, Economy and State, op. cit*, p. 39), "Those activities which are engaged in purely for their own sake are not labor but pure play, consumers' goals in themselves." And in the view of Ludwig von Mises, *Human Action, op. cit.*, pp. 588, 590, "only millionaires choose to remain in their present employment, even though their earnings are now financially insignificant to them."

31. Says Murray Rothbard in this regard, (*Man, Economy and State, op. cit*, p. 39), "Those activities which are engaged in purely for their own sake are not labor but pure play, consumers' goals in themselves." And in the view of Ludwig von Mises, *Human Action, op. cit.*, pp. 588, 590, "only millionaires choose to remain in their present employment, even though their earnings are now financially insignificant to them."

CHAPTER 4

POVERTY

I. INCOME DISTRIBUTION

In the passage of BP which has perhaps been quoted more widely than any other, the bishops state:

> If the United States were a country in which poverty existed amid relatively equitable income distribution, one might argue that we do not have the resources to provide everyone with an adequate living. But, in fact, this is a country marked by glaring disparities of that absolute equality in the distribution of income and wealth is required. Some degree of inequality is not only acceptable, but may be desirable for economic and social reasons. However, gross inequalities are morally unjustifiable, particularly when millions lack even the basic necessities of life. In our judgment, the distribution of income and wealth in the United States is so inequitable that it violates this minimum standard of distributive justice (#202).

There are grave problems with this claim.[1] One difficulty is that equality is a quantitative measure (e.g. the Gini coefficient) and yet the bishops describe it in qualitative terms alone. How could one, even in principle, test the bishops' charge that the U.S. income distribution is inequitable? Suppose the government follows the bishops' advice, and implements their proposals. How shall we know when we have reached that "some degree" of inequity which is not only "acceptable," but even "desirable?" We shall never be able to know it. Therefore, the charge as it now stands is operationally meaningless.

This could of course be easily rectified. All the bishops need do is specify some numerical measure of inequality above which is improper, and below which is proper. But in so doing, they could then open themselves up to the objection of arbitrariness. Why the specified cut off point? Or range? How could it be defended that some measured distributions are "immoral" and others "moral?"

But the chief difficulty is that justice (or injustice) does not properly apply to income distributions. Rather, it applies to the process through which incomes are earned and distributed. If this process is just, whatever results is necessarily proper; if the process is unjust, no possible result can be proper.

Process

Robert Nozick eloquently demonstrates the futility of looking for justice amongst end state theories of income distribution. He has written such a brilliant refutation of all such redistributive schemes, exposing their basic immorality, that his treatment, even though lengthy, deserves to be quoted in full:

> It is not clear how those holding alternative conceptions of distributive justice can reject the entitlement conception of justice in holdings. For suppose a distribution favored by one of these non-entitlement conceptions is realized. Let us suppose it is your favorite one and let us call this distribution D1; perhaps everyone has an equal share, perhaps shares vary in accordance with some dimension you treasure. Now suppose that Wilt Chamberlain is greatly in demand by basketball teams, being a great gate attraction. (Also suppose contracts run only for a year, with players being free agents.) He signs the following sort of contract with a team: In each home game, 25 cents from the price of each ticket of admission goes to him. (We ignore the question of whether he is "gouging" the owners, letting them look out for themselves.) The season starts, and people cheerfully attend his team's games; they buy their tickets, each time dropping a separate 25 cents of their admission price into a special box with Chamberlain's name on it. They are excited about seeing him play; it is worth the total admission price to them. Let us suppose that in one season a million persons attend his home games, and Wilt Chamberlain winds up with $250,000, a much larger sum than the average income and larger even than anyone else has. Is he entitled to this income? Is this new distribution D2, unjust? If so, why? There is *no* question about whether each of the people was entitled to the control over the resources they held in D1; because that was the distribution (your favorite) that (for the purposes of argument) we assumed was acceptable. Each of these persons *choose* to give 25 cents of their money to Chamberlain. They could have spent it on going to the movies, or on candy bars, or on

copies of *Dissent* magazine, or of *Monthly Review*. But they all, at least one million of them, converged on giving it to Wilt Chamberlain in exchange for watching him play basketball. *If D1 was a just distribution, and people voluntarily moved from it to D2, transferring parts of their shares they were given under D1* (what was it for if not to do something with?) *isn't D2 also just?* If the people were entitled to dispose of the resources to which they were entitled (under D1), didn't this include their being entitled to give it to, or exchange it with, Wilt Chamberlain? Can anyone else complain on grounds of justice? Each other person already has his legitimate share under D1. Under D1, there is nothing that anyone has that anyone else has a claim of justice against. After someone transfers something to Wilt Chamberlain, third parties *still* have their legitimate shares; *their* shares are not changed. By what process could such a transfer among two persons give rise to a legitimate claim of distributive justice on a portion of what was transferred, by a third party who had no claim of justice on any holding of the others *before* the transfer? To cut off objections irrelevant here, we might imagine the exchanges occurring in a socialist society, after hours. After playing whatever basketball he does in his daily work, or doing whatever other daily work he does, Wilt Chamberlain decides to put in *overtime* to earn additional money. (First his work quota is set; he works time over that.) Or imagine it is a skilled juggler people like to see, who puts on shows after hours.

Why might someone work overtime in a society in which it is assumed their needs are satisfied? Perhaps because they care about things other than needs. I like to write in books that I read, and to have easy access to books for browsing at odd hours. It would be very pleasant and convenient to have the resources of Widener Library in my back yard. No society, I assume, will provide such resources close to each person who would like them as part of his regular allotment (under D1). Thus, persons either must do without some extra things that they want, or be allowed to do something extra to get some of these things. *On what basis could the inequalities that would eventuate be forbidden?* Notice also that small factories would spring up in a socialist society, unless forbidden. I melt down some of my personal possessions (under D1) and build a machine out of the material. I offer you, and others, a philosophy lecture once a week in exchange for your cranking the handle on my machine, whose products I exchange for yet other things, and so on. (The raw materials used by the machine are given to me by others who possess them under D1, in exchange for hearing lectures.) Each person might participate to gain things over and above their allotment under D1. Some persons even might want to leave their job in socialist industry and work full time in this private sector. I shall say something more about these issues in the next chapter. Here I wish merely to note how private property even in means of production would occur in a socialist society that did not forbid people to use as they wished some of the resources they are given under the socialist distribution D1. The socialist society would have to forbid capitalist acts between consenting adults.

The general point illustrated by the Wilt Chamberlain example and the example of the entrepreneur in a socialist society is that no end-state principle or distributional patterned principle of justice can be continuously realized without continuous interference with people's lives. Any favored pattern would be transformed into one unfavored by the principle, by people choosing to act in various ways; for example, by people exchanging goods and services with other people, or giving things to other people, things the transferrers are entitled to under the favored distributional pattern. *To maintain a pattern one must either continually interfere to stop people from transferring resources as they wish to, or continually (or periodically) interfere to take from some persons resources that others for some reason chose to transfer to them.*[2] (emphasis added)

"Thou shalt not"

While on the subject of morality and forced income transfers in order to equalize the income distribution, we might as well note that a "spade has been called a spade" by some commentators. In their view, "forced income transfers" is nothing better than a prevarication. The blunt but honest translation of this subterfuge is "theft."

States Meinen, under the heading of "Thou shalt not steal:" "Stealing is the taking of what belongs to others against their will. ... theft makes the thief richer and the victim poorer. This transfer of wealth violates the dignity of the thief as a human being and the right to ownership of the victim."[3]

Reed puts matters in the following manner: "the Bible also warns, 'Thou shalt not steal.' It does not say, 'Thou shalt not steal, unless you really need it.' It does not say 'Thou shalt not steal, unless the other guy has more than you do.' It does not say, 'thou shalt not steal, except by majority vote.' *Thou shalt not steal.* Period!"[4]

There is yet another objection to be made of the bishops' call for a redistribution of income within the U.S. It violates not one but two of the principles of BP: the preferential option for the poor, and the idea that we are all God's creatures, no matter which sovereign nation owns our political and citizenship allegiance (#273).

The important thing to realize is that there literally are no poor people in the U.S., poverty line or no poverty line — in the context of poverty

- 40 -

elsewhere in the world. (The bishops are well aware of this fact — see #s 274, 276.) The people at the bottom of the economic pyramid in America would be considered middle class — even upper middle class — if they and their economic lifestyles could be somehow transported to some of the more desperate areas of the world e.g. Ethiopia, Bangladesh, etc. Thus, the call on the part of the bishops for additional wealth transfers from the rich to the poor in the U.S. is — in the global context — really a demand that income be shifted from the wealthy to the middle class. Were there a "preferential option for the middle class," such a policy might conceivably make sense, but it is very difficult, nay impossible, to reconcile it with a preferential option for the *poor*.

So even on the bishops' own grounds, even if it were not immoral to forcibly transfer funds in the manner advocated by the BP, this policy still cannot be justified.

II. REDUCING POVERTY

There are numerous ways to reduce poverty apart from enhancement of the welfare system, upon which the bishops place their greatest reliance.

The BP quite properly launches its discussion of this matter with the most idealistic option. "A key element in removing poverty is prevention through a healthy economy," it states (#209). Fortunately, we have had for the last two hundred years a recipe guaranteed to accomplish that very task. It is Adam Smith's *The Wealth of Nations*. Unfortunately, virtually all of the economic prescriptions given by the bishops are highly incompatible with that volume.

The second point made by the bishops is also very well taken: "Vigorous action should be undertaken to remove barriers to full and equal employment for women and minorities" (#210). But again this is inconsistent with positions taken elsewhere in the BP. Unions, for example, with their seniority systems constitute one of the major barriers against the enhanced employment prospects for women and minority group members. Other road blocks include licensing systems, taxi, truck, bus and other transport regulations, anti-street vendor legislation, and numerous other government interferences with small business.[5] Yet the bishops applaud unions, and do not even consider business deregulation as a means of removing barriers to entry into the labor market.

Next on the list are tax reforms (#s 211, 212). But the priority of BP is for an increase in the progressivity of the tax system, a recommendation certainly at cross purposes with that of promoting a healthy economy.[6] And as Greely so insightfully observes of this emphasis,

In the present context that seems to mean an endorsement of Senator Bill Bradley's (D.-N.J.) bill over Representative Jack Kemp's (R.-N.Y.). I wonder how the bishops can be so sure. The argument for the flat tax, and especially for Congressman Kemp's flat tax, is that progressive tax rates have created a situation in which the tax code has in fact become regressive and that a flat-rate reform will actually increase taxes on the rich because it will be the occasion for destroying the accumulated tax shelters of the ages. Moreover, it would be contended by supporters of the congressman's proposal, progressive rates will always produce such an effect.

My own instincts are with Senator Bradley's three rates; the senator is a Democrat; the congressman's wasp enthusiasm rubs me the wrong way; I did not like the American Football League; and the congressman's son presided over a defeat of my Chicago Bears this year. While the first reason is the main one, I cite the others because it seems to me that the bills are similar enough and the evidence so obscure that one can make a choice between two very similar measures only on instinctual grounds.

Which bill helps the poor more? How can anyone, even a bishop, be so certain as to provide moral and religious support for one and in effect denounce as immoral and irreligious the supporters of the other?[7]

Education

Another proposal points out that "Any long-term solution to the problem of poverty in this country must pay serious attention to education" (#214). True, quite true. The present system of public schooling, especially in the deprived areas of our central cities, is a shame and a disgrace. There, teachers police their charges; very little actual education takes place.[8]

The private Catholic schools are a happy exception to this tale of woe. The bishops "pledge their support" (#215) to this vital institution. But the difficulty is that parents who send their children to Catholic schools must pay double for this privilege: once in tuition fees, and another time in taxes, which go to finance the "education" of other children in the public schools. This, it can be readily appreciated, retards the growth of Catholic schools below the level they would otherwise attain if the competitive process were fair. Why oh why, did the bishops not use this golden opportunity to call for the complete privatization of all public schools? It is to be fervently hoped that this oversight will be corrected in the final draft.

It is of course plain that any such proposal would fly in the face of the bishops' strong reliance on the institutions of government to take upon themselves a greater and greater role in society. The two are in conflict.

But if regard for the state apparatus is great enough to preclude a clarion call for the privatization of education, why is it not also sufficient to convince the bishops to close down all Catholic schools — and thereby to abandon all their students to the tender mercies of the public sector?

III. CHARITY

The bishops' favored means for solving the problem of poverty is, of course, the welfare system. They want more generous payments, national eligibility standards toward this end, an end to the stigma which presently faces recipients (#s 218-240).

Before exploring the drawbacks to these plans, it may be well to consider the appropriate relationship between private charity and government welfare. The bishops leave no doubt that they whole-heartedly support private charitable efforts: "Voluntary donation of money, time and talent to those in need is a Christian imperative arising from God's command that we love our neighbour as ourselves" (#123). However, there is a movement now gaining adherents within the religious community which is at great variance with the bishop's clarion call toward private charity.

In virtually every case where private citizens compete with government, or try to, they do so whole-heartedly. They are anxious to show they can do a better job, at lower cost. Their ultimate aim is to supplant the public sector and to provide the good or service themselves.

This applies, for example, to private sanitation, private bus lines, and even to private competitors for mail delivery, police and fire protection, when such alternatives have arisen.[9]

But there is one glaring exception to this rule: the church-run poverty centers staffed by ideologues who are in the business of providing food for the needy. They are highly ambivalent about their role. According to spokespersons from such groups, giving food to the poor should really be a government enterprise. In the good society, in the view of these people, there would be little scope for private initiatives such as their own; the public sector should do the job. They even go so far as to claim that the government, whenever it decreases welfare payments, is taking advantage of the "kindly and loving" people, such as themselves, who minister to the poor. They let it be clearly known that they have no intention of expanding their base of operation to take up any slack left by government. According to the Right Reverend Robert Smith, moderator of the United Church of Canada, for example, all those who support private food banks are not really engaging in an act of Christian charity. Rather, they are "prolonging the agony" of the poor, and "letting government off the hook."[10]

- 43 -

Loaves and fishes

This is a rather peculiar view. Does it mean that when Jesus Christ performed the miracle of the loaves and the fishes, He was not really undertaking an act of Christian charity, but was instead acting as a sort of shill for the Romans, the government of the day? The very idea is preposterous and ludicrous. Yet, such a conclusion is the one forced upon us by the "logic" of Reverend Smith's remarks.

All of this is in sharp contrast to the views of the old time, long-term private groups which have been on the scene for decades. Organization such as the Salvation Army, the Union Gospel Missions, and the Sisters of Atonement Mission. In sharp contrast, in the view of these more traditional groups, their main purpose is to feed the hungry and spread the gospel — that's what Jesus Christ was all about. For them, it doesn't depend on what the government does or does not do.

The bishops might consider clarifying their position on this matter in their final draft. They favor private charity, but if government reduces welfare, do they stand with those traditional groups who are ready and eager to "take up the slack?" Or shall the Catholic Church in the U.S. make common cause with those who not only refuse to expand the traditional role of religious organizations in charitable work, but who advocate actual abdication?[11]

IV. WELFARE

We come now to the welfare program, the system upon which the bishops place their prime emphasis as an antidote to poverty.

Let us then consider in some detail the precise nature of this policy, and the devastation it has wreaked on an entire generation and more of American citizens.

By any relevant measure — crime, incarceration, illegitimacy, scholastic aptitude tests, unemployment, dependency — the poor in the U.S. were worse off in 1980 than they were in 1950, after 30 years of the "golden age" of welfare.[12] The problem, at least for the economist, can be summarized by the phrase "upward sloping supply curves." This means that if people are offered more money provided they exhibit a certain characteristic — even poverty, as in this case — they will tend to act so as to supply a greater amount of this characteristic. If the rewards are sufficient, people will reorient their entire lives.

For example, says George Gilder:

> The welfare system makes an irresistible offer to every eligible female over the age of 16 ... it says to every black female teenager, 'You may be poor, you may have family problems, and you may be discouraged about your future. But if you have a baby right now, we will give you your own apartment, free medical care, food stamps, and a regular income over the next 20 years. If you have another baby soon after, we will increase your allotment.'
>
> How many black men — poor or affluent — can match that offer? How many teenage girls *anywhere* — black or white, poor or affluent — can afford their *own apartment* and pay their *own medical expenses* at age 16?
>
> These teenage girls who drop out of school and have babies are not ignorant, they are not morally weak, and they are not sexually lascivious. They are simply rational human beings making the most intelligent choice on how to improve their economic condition.[13]

This is why, finds Tucker, that "every year more black girls drop out of high school to have a baby than graduate from college."[14]

A refutation?

But the bishops do not accept this argument. In their view "These mothers are also accused of having more children so that they can raise their allowances. The truth is that 70 percent of AFDC families have only one or two children, and that there is little financial advantage in having another" (#225).

This seems like a refutation of Tucker, but it is not. Note the equivocation between the "a baby" mentioned by Tucker and the "more children" alluded to by the bishops. The point is, both are correct. Neither is contrary to the other. The welfare greatly encourages black female teens to have one or two babies, but not necessarily many more.

And this program has played havoc with family formation in the inner cities. In an analysis which might have been addressed to the authors of BP (except that it was published earlier), Tucker states:

> What was completely missing is the understanding that black families are not really 'breaking up' at all. Instead, *black families are no longer forming*. When women start 'families,' they no longer look for a husband. They simply marry the state.
>
> What black women are discovering is one of those inherent biological truths long suppressed by social conventions. When you get right down

to it, for a woman who wants to have a baby, the whole business of finding a husband to support her while she takes care of the children (or to take care of the children while she supports them) is really a tedious, potentially fruitless, undertaking. If the government can make a better offer, why refuse it? What's a few hours waiting in welfare lines, compared to a lifetime of having to put up with an unpredictable emotionally draining, potentially violent man?

In reality, the 'black family' is not 'breaking up' at all. It is simply kicking black men out of the house and taking in the government as the breadwinner.''

Weak family?

But has not the black family always been weak, perhaps as part of the ''legacy of slavery?'' Not at all. Continues Tucker

> ... contrary to all the banter about contemporary black family problems being the 'legacy of slavery' or a 'product of African institutions,' black nuclear families actually remained heroically intact, not only through slavery, but right through the backlash against Reconstruction and into the early years of the twentieth century.
>
> The black family was more than strong enough to survive the ordeal of slavery ... (there are) tragic accounts of black men and women walking up and down the countryside after the Civil War searching for wives, husbands, or children from whom they had become separated during the chaos of the conflict. Advertisements for lost spouses and children were still appearing in black newspapers as late as the 1880s ... Black social patterns were ruined only when liberals arrived on the scene in the 1930s with their 'Aid to Families With Dependent Children' and other blandishments to 'let the state do for people what they aren't capable of doing for themselves.' The tragedy occurred because blacks *trusted* the system. They didn't have the inherent suspicions to resist government assistance and avoid sympathetic bureaucrats like the plague — as many ethnic groups did then and still do today ... No, the black family was more than strong enough to survive slavery. It was just not strong enough to survive the welfare system.[15]

When the bishops advocate that ''public assistance programs should be adequately funded and provide recipients with decent support'' (#227) they are unwittingly encouraging a diabolical plan that has been the utter ruination of many poor people. In fact, had one set out purposefully to ruin the black family structure, a better plan than the present welfare system could hardly be devised. When the bishops urge that ''public-assistance programs should strengthen rather than weaken marriage and the family'' (#231) they are in effect asking water to run uphill, requesting thunder without lightening, and, not to put too fine a point on it, asking that 2 plus 2 cease to equal 4.

What program might be erected in the place of this morally bankrupt system? Alternatively, upon what different policy ought our primary interests be centered, leaving government welfare as an absolute last resort, should all else fail?

The answer is obvious: our substitute ought to be reliance on private charity, which has traditionally been organized and carried out by religious institutions.

The mormons

Consider the Mormon system of aiding its own poor.[16] Its aim is to abolish idleness (to which is very definitely attached a stigma, contrary to the BP, (#220, 222, 225, 236, 237) and to encourage independence, industry, thrift and self-respect. How is this done? By placing work and self-help at the center of the program. The Mormon Welfare Plan specifically provides that people work within the program on Church properties, if need be, if employment for them cannot be found elsewhere. Notice just how sharply divergent is this philosophy from that of the bishops, who state

> Eligibility for public assistance should also not depend on work requirements or work tests. There is little or no evidence that people need to be compelled to work, and therefore there is no good reason to subject them to such tests. Assignment to unpaid work in the form of 'workfare' is a particularly objectionable requirement for welfare. All work should be fairly compensated so that workers receive the full benefits and status associated with gainful employment (#235).

Certainly there is "no evidence that people need to be compelled to work,'' but the upward-slopingness of supply curves is one of the most empirically established findings in all of economics. And this indicates that the greater are the rewards for work (or for anything else) the more effort will be expended in order to attain these rewards. Tying work to rewards, for those who wish assistance, is only demeaning for those who wish something for nothing.

Part and parcel of the bishops' denial of the fact that supply curves slope in an upward direction is their claim that personal motivation is irrelevant to poverty (#193). And if motivation has nothing to do with being in dire economic straights, neither can laziness (#222). Stated so baldly, it is not easy to comprehend how the bishops could have boxed themselves into a position so much at odds with common sense.

We would expect that such an indefensible claim would be seized upon by the critics. And in the event, we are not disappointed. Complains Hitchcock, ''... there is practically no discussion in the episcopal letter of the role of free choice or enterprising action in alleviating economic distress.''[17] And states Wolfe, ''The causes of poverty certainly include many of the factors that the draft cites, but the arbitrary exclusion of motivation as a possible factor seems unjustified.''[18]

The poverty line

We turn now to a discussion of the poverty line, an issue that looms large in the treatment of this question in the BP.

It is clear that the bishops' assessment of poverty in the U.S. is based on official government definitions of poverty (#187). But this is a relative, not an absolute measure of standards of living.[19] The cut off point of $10,000 for a non-farm family of four in 1984, is hardly the dividing line between physical sustenance and penury. By international standards this is affluence, not deprivation.[20] True, there are food lines and soup kitchens all across the country (#188). But this is only testimonial to the fact that numerous people are willing to accept items of value if offered for free.[21]

The BP warns that ''the effects of improper nutrition are particularly damaging to small children ...'' (#188) and this is certainly true, but the implication that this is related to poverty in America is not valid. George Stigler has calculated that an expense of only $8 per month would be sufficient to provide a family of four with sufficient nutrients to maintain health.[22] No, the reasons for improper nutrition will have to be sought elsewhere, arguably in realms the bishops ask us to avoid, lest they lead to stereotypes and stigmas.

Negative income tax

We shall conclude our discussion by considering one additional reason for opposing the expansion of the welfare system. In order to do so, we shall accept for the sake of argument each and every one of the premises set out in the BP, stated or implied: that the poverty line is a meaningful measure of distress; that the length of soup lines provide a reasonable indication of poverty; that international comparisons are irrelevant for questions of domestic welfare; that relative poverty, not the absolute variety, is the proper basis for public policy; that what matters for justice is not process, but end state; that there is a readily definable amount of equality that is acceptable, but that the present income and wealth distribution is ''immoral'' for not attaining this level; that forced income redistribution does not amount to theft and thus is not proscribed by the Bible; that neither private charity — nor a vast improvement in the economy — can be relied upon to solve the problem of poverty; and that the present welfare system is not responsible for the destabilization of the family and other aspects of social disarray.

Even given all these premises, it still does not follow that expansion of the present welfare system is justified. For there is still one other option that may satisfy the bishops' wishes to an even greater degree: the negative income tax.[23]

According to this plan, some income cut off point is selected. If income in excess of this level is earned, positive taxes are paid (from the citizen to the government). But if earnings fall below this limit, negative income taxes are paid, i.e. subsidies are received by the poor person from the public treasury.

The case worker

One major benefit of this proposal is that it cuts out the "welfare middle man," the case worker. This should be entirely welcome to the authors of BP since the welfare-dispensing bureaucrat is the person primarily responsible for imposing "surveillance" on the poor, and "using regulations to create difficulties for clients and otherwise showing the poor that they are not to be trusted" (#238). With the negative income tax, the person in "poverty" need only file the return in the mail, in the same manner as any other taxpayer — a result surely to be warmly welcomed by the bishops.[24] Could the reason the authors of BP have not embraced this policy be that it was first proposed by Milton Friedman? He is a Nobel prize-winning economist who has intensively studied this problem, but is never even cited in the voluminous bibliography of the BP.

One further benefit is that vast sums of money could be saved. It is estimated that "more money is actually spent directly on the poor each year (more than $100 billion) than would be required, if distributed directly to the poor, to lift every man, woman and child among them above the poverty level. That this has not actually been achieved is *prima facie* evidence of faulty design in poverty programs."[25] Further, "a mere $45 billion would lift all poor persons in the U.S. above the poverty line."[26]

V. DISCRIMINATION

A major cause of poverty, say the bishops, is discrimination; both racial and ethnic (#s 196,197) and sexual (#s 198-201). This claim, however, is very much at odds with the findings of the best research on the subject.

Consider first racial and ethnic discrimination. It is only possible to infer discrimination as a source of different incomes if ethnic groups are indistinguishable from each other in all other regards. It is impossible to measure, and certainly to quantify, characteristics such as determination, motivation, perseverance, which have an obvious influence on earnings. But with regard to variables more conducive to measurement, it is easy to demonstrate that all ethnic groups are far from alike in dimensions associated with income levels.

Let us take age, for example. One need not resort to discrimination as an explanation as to why Jewish, Polish, Italian or German earnings should be far in excess of those of Mexicans, Puerto Ricans, Blacks or Indians. The former groups are composed mainly of adults, in peak income years; the latter, relatively, of children. For example, over 40 percent of Polish Americans have reached their fourth decade, while this holds true for only 20 percent of American Indians, Mexican Americans or Puerto Ricans. The same pattern prevails when one considers only the age of the adult population: Puerto-Rican income-earning heads of families were 36 years old on average, while the corresponding age for Jews was 50.

Median Ages and Family Incomes of American Ethnic Groups (1970)

Ethnicity	Age	Income as Percentage of National Average
Jewish	46	172
Japanese	32	132
Polish	40	115
Chinese	27	112
Italian	16	112
German	36	107
Anglo Saxon	(NA)	105
Irish	37	102
National Average	28	100
Filipino	(NA)	99
West Indian	(NA)	94
Mexican	18	76
Puerto Rican	18	63
Black	22	62
Indian	20	60

Source: Thomas Sowell[27]

As can be seen from the accompanying table, with the exception of Chinese Americans, all ethnic groups with earnings above the national average were older than the citizenry at large, while all those with below average incomes were younger. As well, a similar pattern holds with regard to age of marriage, number of children, quantity and quality of education, geographical location, skills, training, continuity in the labor force: those groups at the bottom of the economic pyramid were also disadvantaged in each of these other characteristics.[28]

A paradox

Of particular relevance to the Sowell thesis (ethnic income disparities can best be explained by different group characteristics, not by discrimination) is that Jewish-, Chinese-, and Japanese-Americans have been victimized by some of the most vicious discrimination in U.S. history, and yet may be found at the top of the ethnic income distribution. Even more revealing, perhaps, is the case of West Indians who have moved to the U.S. Although physically indistinguishable from black Americans, their incomes are 94 percent of the national average, compared to the 62 percent registered by the latter group (see table). What accounts for this sharp income disparity? Sowell attributes it to differences in culture and motivation: a greater emphasis on hard work, learning, schooling, etc., on the part of the West Indians.

But perhaps racist American employers are more subtle than we give them "credit" for, and discriminate not only on the basis of skin colour, but also because of accent, birthplace and country of childhood — here the black Americans and first generation West Indian immigrants can be distinguished — and that this accounts for the differing earning experiences of the two groups. There are problems with this view, however. First, why should the racists discriminate more against either group, relative to the other? And second, Sowell tells us, second generation West Indians — who are indistinguishable from black Americans with regard to accent, origin, etc. — earn even more than their first generation predecessors, and not only more than the national average, but more than Anglo Saxons as well!

Sexism

Now let us consider the bishops' views concerning the feminization of poverty. They state that "... women who work outside their homes full time and year-around earn only 61 percent of what men earn" and that "... women suffer outright discrimination, in wages, salaries, job classifications, promotions and other areas" (#s 199,201).

But just as discrimination plays little if any role in explaining ethnic income differences, neither can it account for the compensation gap between men and women. Yes, females earn only some three-fifths of what males do, but this figure, paradoxically, hides more than it reveals.

It is marital status, not employer discrimination, which accounts for the 61 percent figure, i.e., for the 39 percent "gap." When the population is divided up by marital status, separating those who have never been married from all others (the married, widowed, divorced, separated) it turns out that the female/male income ratio for the former group approaches unity, while that for the latter group is much below the 61 percent level posted for the entire society.[29]

The bishops had the perspicacity to see the importance of marriage, child rearing, housework for earnings. They recognize that "women continue to have primary responsibility for childbearing" (#200) and that "women often anticipate that they will leave the labor force to have and raise children, and often make job and career choices accordingly" (#201). But even they fail to appreciate the utterly enormous effects this phenomena can have on the relative earnings of men and women.

Asymmetry

Marriage has an asymmetrical effect on male and female incomes, enhancing the former, and reducing the latter. And the reasons for this are legion. Not only are child rearing and housework tasks unevenly shared, but there are several other factors which exacerbate this divergence in earnings. For example, married women refuse promotions and wage increases on the grounds that this will threaten their relationships,[30] and families make locational decisions in order to increase the income potentiality of the husband, not the wife.[31]

Indeed, the very idea that employer discrimination could account for a female-male earnings ratio of 61 percent, as alleged by the bishops, is illogical. For suppose that a sexist employer were confronted with two job candidates, a man and a woman, whose productivity levels were identical at $10 per hour. (We must assume equal productivity; otherwise unequal wages can be attributed to that factor, and not to sexism.) Further suppose that in accordance with the fiction of 61 percent, the going wage for males was $10 per hour and that for women was an hourly $6.10. Then it would be as if the female job applicant had a little sign on her person stating, "Hire me instead of him and you shall earn an additional profit of $3.90 per hour." What sexist employer could resist such a temptation? And if he did, how long could he remain in business, in view of the fact that his competitors would be delighted to grab up a bargain of such monumental proportions?[32]

Notes

1. A minor shortcoming is that the bishops base their abhorrence of the present income distribution on the understanding that "in 1982 the richest 20% of Americans received more income than the bottom 70% combined and nearly as much as all other Americans combined. The poorest 20% of the people received only about 4% of the nation's income while the poorest 40% received only 13%" (#202). But these calculations ignore the value of non-cash benefits to the poor, thus biasing their figures toward greater inequality. See 23, p. 13; also see 15, p. 18, footnote 6 for a further correction on the bishops' calculations of wealth distribution.

2. *Anarchy, State and Utopia, op. cit.*, pp. 160-163; Paul Heyne also makes this vital moral distinction between process and end state. Says he: "The justice or injustice of a social system will not be found in the patterns of outcomes it yields — its end states — but in the procedures through which those end states emerge." See 15, p. 10. It should be noted, however, that several of the bishops' critics incorrectly accept their equation of a more equal income distribution with morality. See, for example, 23, p. 13, where the degree of income equality which has been attained in the U.S. is seen as a "significant achievement."

3. See 21, p. 1.

4. See p. 28, p. 2. The Lay Letter appears unable to clearly distinguish between charity, benevolence and generosity on the one hand, and forced income transfers, or theft, on the other. It states, "The generosity of the American people in wishing to help the poor by supporting legislation specifically targeted on the needs of the poor ... has been immense" (see 25, p. 59). But this is mistaken. The truly magnificent generosity of the American people cannot be seen in the welfare system; rather, it is based on the huge private charitable donations which have been given. See in this regard H. Geoffrey Brennan, "Markets and Majorities, Morals and Madness: An Essay on Religion and Institutional Choice," in *Morality of the Market: Religious and Economic Perspectives*, Walter Block, H. Geoffrey Brennan and Kenneth Elzinga, eds., Vancouver: The Fraser Institute, 1985; for evidence that the American welfare system has hurt, not helped, the poor, see Charles Murray, *Losing Ground, op. cit.*

5. See Walter Williams, *The State Against Blacks, op. cit.*; also "Negro Group is Ordered to Halt Bus Service Here," *New York Times* (January 3, 1968), p. 36; "Negro Group Seeks to Buy City Buses," *New York Times* (January 4, 1968), p. 27, which describes the plight of the National Economic Growth and Reconstruction Organization (N.E.G.R.O.), which was ordered to stop operating an unfranchised bus service in Queens, New York; "Negro Bus Line Enjoined," *New York Times* (January 5, 1968), p. 32: "Where Blacks Own the Bus," *Business Week* (May 15, 1971), p. 78.

6. See *Taxation: An International Perspective*, Walter Block and Michael Walker, eds., Vancouver: The Fraser Institute, 1984.

7. See 14, p. 34.

8. Paul Avrich, *The Modern School Movement*, Princeton University Press, 1980; *Education in a Free Society*, Anne Husted Burleigh, ed., Indianapolis: Liberty Press, 1973; *The Public School Monopoly: A Critical Analysis of Education and the State in American Society*, Robert B. Everhart, ed., New York: Harper and Row, 1983.

9. Murray N. Rothbard, *For a New Liberty*, New York: MacMillan, 1973; William C. Woolridge, *Uncle Sam the Monopoly Man*, New Rochelle, N.Y.: Arlington House, 1970; Robert Poole, *Cutting Back City Hall*, New York: Universe Books, 1980.

10. See *The Vancouver Sun*, June 22, 1985, p. A1.

11. The prognostication does not look too good. There are, unfortunately, indications that were the bishops to expound on this issue, they would come down on the side of those who wish government to usurp the charitable role of religious institutions. See 7, p. 247; 12, p. 349; 35, p. 12. Most ominous is the bishops' statement, "The works of charity cannot and should not have to substitute for humane public policy" (#208).

12. Must reading on welfare includes: Charles Murray, *Losing Ground: American Social Policy 1950-1980*, N.Y.: Basic Books, 1985; George Gilder, *Wealth and Poverty*, N.Y.: Basic Books, 1981; Edward Banfield, *The Unheavenly City Revisited, op. cit.*; Thomas Sowell, *The Economics and Politics of Race; idem., Knowledge and Decisions*; Martin Anderson, *Welfare*, Hoover Institution, 1978; Henry Hazlitt, *The Conquest of Poverty*, N.Y.: Arlington House, 1973; Irving Kristol, *Two Cheers for Capitalism*, New York, Basic Books, 1978; and a short brilliant piece that deserves more attention than it has so far received, William Tucker, "Black Family Agonistes," *The American Spectator*, Vol. 17, No. 7, July 1984, pp. 14-17.

13. George Gilder, *Visible Man*, cited by Tucker, p. 15.

14. Tucker, *op. cit.*, p. 15.

15. *Ibid.*, p. 16.

16. See "Welfare Plan of the Church of Jesus Christ of Latter-Day Saints," Salt Lake City: The General Church Welfare Committee, 1960, cited in Murray N. Rothbard, *For a New Liberty, op. cit.*

17. See 16, p. 8.

18. See 39, p.11.

19. See 3, p. 32.

20. See Sowell, *The Economics and Politics of Race, op. cit.*, p.21.

21. When banks give out toasters, clocks, and radios in order to attract new depositors, and there are line-ups around the block in order to take advantage of these offers, this does not mean that these wealthy savers were toaster-, clock-, or radio-deprived. In like manner, queues at soup kitchens do not necessarily imply abject hunger.

22. George Stigler, *The Theory of Price*, *op. cit.*, p. 2; see also *idem.*, "The Cost of Subsistence," *Journal of Farm Economics*, XXVII, 1945, pp. 303-314. In terms of November 1985 dollars, $8 per month equals $32.96 per month.

23. Milton Friedman, *Capitalism and Freedom, op. cit.*

24. To be sure there are also many and strenuous objections to the negative income tax on moral and practical grounds. In addition to all those listed above which apply to the welfare system, the negative income tax has the following two defects; first, in removing the "stigma" and "stereotypes" of welfare, it opens the floodgates of forced income redistribution even the more; now, no one need hold back from accepting the largesse out of a sense of pride, for example; secondly, the negative income is more compatible with the discredible doctrine of positive "rights" or welfare "rights" than is public assistance as presently constituted.

25. See 25, p. 59; see also 29, p. 7.

26. See 24, p. 14.

27. Thomas Sowell, "Presuppositions of Affirmative Action," in *Discrimination, Affirmative Action and Equal Opportunity, op. cit.*; also see note 98, supra. This data is for the 1970 census, based on 1969 incomes which were compiled two years *before* the advent of federal guidelines mandating "affirmative actions" and thus cannot be accounted for on the basis of the policy.

28. See Thomas Sowell, *Ethnic America: A History*, N.Y.: Basic Books, 1981; *idem.*, *Civil Rights: Rhetoric or Reality?*, N.Y.: William Morrow, 1984; *idem.*, *Essays and Data on American Ethnic Groups*, ed., Washington, D.C.: Urban Institute, 1978; *idem.*, *The Economics and Politics of Race*, N.Y.: William Morrow, 1983; *idem.*, *Pink and Brown People*, Stanford: Hoover Institution, 1981. It is almost an understatement to say that Thomas Sowell is the world's pre-eminent authority in discrimination, black poverty, ethnicity, affirmative action and related subjects. His omission as a consultant to the bishops is thus as serious as it is inexplicable. It is hoped that this will be rectified before the next draft of BP sees the light of day.

29. Thomas Sowell found that "as of 1971, single women in their thirties who had worked continuously since leaving school earned slightly more than single men of the same age, even though women as a group earned slightly less than half as much as men as a group. In the academic world, single female faculty members who had received their Ph.D.s in the 1930s had by the 1950s become full professors to a slightly greater extent than male Ph.D.s of the same vintage, even though female academics who never married earned more than male academics who never married, even before 'affirmative action' 'goals and timetables' became mandatory in 1971''; in "Presuppositions of Affirmative Action," *op. cit.*, p. 51; Block calculated female/male income ratios for Canada also in 1971, and reported them as follows; for the total population, 37.4 percent, for those who were ever married, 33.2 percent for those who were never married, 99.2

percent, *ibid.*, p. 112; and Walter Block and Michael Walker, *Focus: On Employment Equity: A Critique of the Abella Royal Commission Report*, Vancouver: The Fraser Institute, 1985, pp. 48, 50-51, uncovered for 1971 a female/male income ratio of 109.8 percent for never-married Canadians with a university degree. The comparable figures for ever married with a university degree was 56.8 percent and for the total population educated at this level, 61.2 percent.

30. See Block, "Economic Intervention, Discrimination and Unforeseen Consequences," in *Discrimination, Affirmative Action, op. cit.*, footnote 2, pp. 246-248; Carl Hoffman and John Reed, "When Is Imbalance Not Discrimination," *ibid.*, pp. 183-216; Block and Walker, *Employment Equity, ibid.*, p. 38.

31. *Ibid.*, Hoffman and Reed; Block and Walker, *Employment Equity, ibid.* p. 39.

32. Another fallacious implication of the employer discrimination hypothesis is that industries and firms which employ (exploit) the most women would earn the greatest profits, and those which hire the fewest (exploit women the least) would earn the lowest profits. But this is untenable, as there is a powerful force in the marketplace which tends to equate profits in all lines of endeavour; capitalists continually shuffle their investments in the direction of the greatest returns (tending to lower them) and away from those areas which have the poorest profit records (tending to improve them). See Block & Walker, *Employment Equity, op. cit.*, pp. 60-62.

CHAPTER 5

ECONOMIC COLLABORATION

I. COOPERATION

It is not a difficult task to recognize direct or explicit cooperation. Food co-ops, housing cooperatives, barn raisings, the kibbutz, two people carrying a package too heavy for either one alone — all are instances of cooperation that are well known, and easily identifiable as such.

It is far more difficult to appreciate cooperation when it appears in conjunction with competitive exercises. As I write, Karpov and Kasparov are engaged in a highly competitive struggle to determine which of them shall be the world champion chess player. The competitiveness between these two men is clearly visible.

But there is also cooperation at work here. The two of them together are cooperating in creating something which, at least in the eyes of chess aficionados, will be nothing less than a work of art.

If one of these two combatants should suddenly lose his ability, there would no longer be any competition. The other would crush him. But there would be no cooperation (or very little) either. No longer could their game be considered a thing of beauty. Now it would just be a gifted grandmaster giving a chess lesson to a "wood pusher." Their competitive struggle in this seemingly paradoxical sense is no less cooperative than the co-authorship of a novel. or the playing of a Mozart duet, or of the interaction between the eight participants in a rowing shell.

Economic instruction

If it is hard to see a cooperative element in explicitly competitive games, it is even more difficult to see how any such thing can possibly take place in a free market economy. But it is probably only a slight exaggeration to say that the main and indeed only task of the instructor of economics is to teach his beginning students precisely this lesson. If the professor succeeds, he will have imparted a good grounding in the subject to his charges, even if that is the only thing he does. If he fails in this one goal, his students will still be economically illiterate, no matter to what other exotica they may have been introduced.

It is perhaps for this reason that Paul Heyne makes this the central point in his critique of BP. Heyne brilliantly points to the crux of the bishops' failure to comprehend how the market can coordinate the individual plans of millions of Americans:

> The bishops' defense of private property probably provides the most revealing evidence of their failure to understand the role of relative prices. Private ownership of property, they say, has value for many reasons. Four are then given. It provides incentives for diligence, allows parents to contribute to the welfare of their children, protects political liberty, and opens space for the exercise of creativity and initiatives (#120). Economists will point to a glaring omission from this list: clearly defined and readily exchangeable property rights generate relative prices that offer information on the prospective net advantage of alternative decisions, thereby providing an essential part of the society's system of coordination.
>
> Those who fail to recognize the role of prices as coordinating signals almost always fail to notice that markets are mechanisms of social coordination. Thus the bishops believe that 'economic freedom, personal initiative and the free market,' though 'deservedly esteemed in our society,' are at odds with the 'inescapably social and political nature of the economy' (#256). They see only the individualistic aspect of market activity, but never its cooperative and coordinative side.
>
> Since markets don't coordinate, by their assumptions, it is essential that 'society make provision for overall planning in the economic domain' (#260, quoting Pope John Paul II). What this means is that 'all actors of society, including government, must actively and positively cooperate in forming national economic policies' (#263). These last words are italicized, suggesting that they are intended to comprise more than a mere truism. But what can they possibly mean? Perhaps committees charged with producing a cooperative report start to turn out meaningless pleas for cooperation as they grow more weary in their search for consensus.
>
> 'We are well aware,' the *Letter* states, 'that the mere mention of the notion of economic planning is likely to produce a violent allergic reaction in U.S. society' (#261). Perhaps it will. But the bishops' discussion of planning is also likely to produce some 'violent' reactions on

the part of people who think it's time to retire the claim that a market economy is an 'unplanned' economy. The *Letter* reveals no understanding at all of what effective economic planning requires or of how the U.S. economy is in fact coordinated.[1]

How, then, can relative prices help people cooperate through the intermediation of the marketplace?

Dieting

Let us take as an example a problem that has afflicted an increasingly prosperous society such as ours. People suddenly decide they are too fat, and decide to go on a diet. For simplicity, we assume that this means they will demand more celery and less cake.

Do the people in such a case have to appeal to their elected leaders? Must they hold public meetings with farmers, bakers, confectioners, supermarkets, and other groups without whose cooperation their changed plans cannot be put into effect? Must they appeal in such meetings to the public spiritedness (or "corporate responsibility") of the people who must "participate" in any such decision?

Of course not. The people merely go out into the market and purchase more celery and fewer cakes. This one simple elemental economic activity — through the "magic of the marketplace"[2] — sets a whole train of events into motion, all of which may be viewed as inducing other people to cooperate with the dieters.

The switch in buying patterns will leave unsold cakes on the shelves, and empty them of celery. This, in turn, will discourage entrepreneurs from the production of the former and divert them to the latter. Complementary and substitute goods will also be affected. For example, salad dressings will have been given a shot in the arm, while coffee (as in coffee'n'cake) will take a nose dive. Still further reverberations will take place, as when a stone is thrown into a quiet pool, and the waves interact in complex ways. It will now be less likely that land suitable for the growing of celery will be converted for residential, commercial or industrial use, while sugar beet farms, and lands upon which sugar cane, wheat, eggs and other ingredients of cakes are produced, are more likely to be condemned for these purposes.

At every step of the way in this process, it is the profit and loss system[3] which gives the appropriate incentives, so that it is in the interests of people to do those things which promote the plans of the dieters, or to refrain from doing that which is discoordinative with them. True, businessmen can act in an uncooperative manner, either from sheer cursedness, inadvertence, or from lack of knowledge. But if they conduct their enterprises in such

- 59 -

a way, they tend to lose customers, suffer losses, and must eventually go bankrupt. It is these rewards and penalties which tend to ensure that the competitive system remains essentially a cooperative one.

With this introduction to the subject, we are now ready to analyze the misunderstandings of the marketplace, which underlie the call for explicit (i.e., government) planning, coordination, cooperation, or collaboration.

II. ECONOMIC DEMOCRACY

The bishops launch their advocacy of "economic democracy" on the grounds that as the U.S. represents a new and better experiment and a new and improved direction in political democracy, so it must now do for the economic sphere what it has already accomplished in the political.[4] Apart from the idea which underlies this initiative, even the choice of name is unfortunate. For "economic democracy" is widely known in the U.S. as the political philosophy of Jane Fonda and Tom Hayden, and of the left-leaning Institute for Policy Studies, and in Europe as the guiding light of a number of avowedly socialist organizations.[5]

But the idea itself is even worse. It is predicated, first, on the view that cooperation and conciliation can occur in the political arena, but not in the marketplace;[6] but this, as we have seen, is erroneous. If anything, there is more cooperation in the free enterprise system, albeit only implicitly, than there is in politics, which is presumably organized to this end.

Then, there are the disanalogies between politics and economics. In western industrialized nations such as the U.S., it is a basic premise that every person shall have one vote. That is, political power shall be equalized, at least in theory. Were this applied holus bolus to the economic sphere, the implication would be an absolute equalization of wealth, i.e., economic power would be exactly the same for all. This may well be the intention of some of the advocates of "economic democracy," but it is hardly one they could afford to publicize for it would lead only to equal immizeration of the populace. There is the further difficulty that were we all to vote (political-ballot-box-wise) on economic issues, we would be voting on the allocation of the property of other people. True economic democracy would mean, for example, that Mr. Jones could not alone determine the usage of his own automobile, home, or even his shoes and socks. Rather, all of us, "we the people," would have a share in such decision-making. But were such a procedure to actually take place, it would mean the end to all private property as we have known it.[7]

III. PARTICIPATION

The BP ofttimes expresses its concern for the implementation of cooperation under the rubric of "participation" (see #s 92,94,95,104). The claim is sometimes made that by the very fact of our membership in the human race, we are all entitled to participate in the decisions which affect our lives.[8]

But there are grave drawbacks in this view. One problem is that in a large complex and interconnected society such as ours, we are all quite literally dependent upon millions of decisions made by thousands and thousands of others who take part in the economy. To take a rather plebian example, the quality of all of our lives depends in no small part on the price of our homes. But housing prices are a function of the choices of people as disparate as loggers, plumbers, roofers, tree planters, brickmakers, electricians, architects — the list could go on and on. Are we each to demand a right to have an input into the entire decision-making processes of all such people who can effect housing prices? The very idea is ludicrous.[9]

Another difficulty with this call for participation is that it ignores the role played by the consumers in a free economy. As we have seen in the case of the dieters, the purchasers of goods can and do "participate" in the economy in a very meaningful manner. In fact, they exercise no less than a thumbs up or thumbs down veto power over the offerings of entrepreneurs. It is due to the participation (in a negative sense) of the customers in the U.S. that such items as the Edsel, the hula hoop and the beanie are no longer selling in great numbers. The manufacturers of these goods would be only too happy if the people responsible for their losses of profits were not able to exercise their rights of participation in this regard.

IV. "BALANCED" CENTRAL PLANNING

When governmental central planning was first proposed, it was done so on the grounds of rationality. The marketplace, it was thought, could not rationally plan, since it consisted of thousands and even millions of individuals; what was needed for coherent economic activity, in this view, was the vision of a single planner or, at most, a small committee of experts, who could sit around a large table, compare notes, and come up with a blueprint for the entire society.

But then the reaction set in. Economists pointed out that although the market could boast of no single rational thought process which undergirded the entire system, it was still planned intelligently.[10] This was because even though the market consisted of the activities of millions of entrepreneurs, these individuals were not forced to act independently of each other, in chaotic confusion. Rather, they were linked together by a powerful informational system: that of prices, profits and losses.

Now, enter the bishops into this intellectual fray. The BP is too wise to play the gambit with which the debate began. That is, it refrains from claiming that only central planning can be rational. It specifically concedes that "Individuals plan" (#262). Instead, the bishops take a different tack. They call for "balance" between the planning of individuals, coordinated through markets, and that of governments, which is done explicitly, through the good offices of bureaucrats. (The call for "balance" is a continual refrain in the BP, and may be found in #s 259-263, 297, 323.)

But this clearly will not do. If the bishops are to justify their call for balance, they shall have to do so on the grounds that the "unbalanced" system of individual planning coordinated through the market is somehow objectionable. That is to say, they shall have to enter the socialist calculation debate (which is happily ignored in the BP), and take a position somewhere between that of Taylor and Lange (socialism) on the one hand, and that of Mises and Hayek (capitalism) on the other. Otherwise, their appeal for balance is just a recommendation based on no foundation.

Unfortunately, the bishops fail to make any case of the sort. Their clarion call for balance rests only on a general presumption in favor of compromise, perhaps deriving from the Aristotelian "golden mean."[11]

V. EMPLOYEE STOCK OWNERSHIP PLANS

So minute and detailed are the recommendations of the BP regarding the economy that it even defends employee stock ownership plans. State the bishops: "Management and workers should develop new forms of partnership and cooperation, such as cooperative ownership and worker participation in ownership and decision making."[12]

Why encourage the workers to take on an ownership role, to become, as it were, capitalists on a small scale? The idea seems to have been initiated by the work of Louis Kelso,[13] who advocated employee stock ownership plans as a way of saving the capitalist system. He was impressed by the notion that if the workers had a stake in the marketplace, through their ownership of corporate stock, they would become firm supporters, as new members of the capitalist class; as well, he contended, this would achieve gains in labor productivity, further cementing their adherence of this system.

But this raises numerous questions. To begin with, even if the bishops share the Kelsonian analysis, it is difficult to understand why they would employ it. For the saving of the capitalist system could hardly be considered a prime objective of the BP, and this initiative is surely a sharp departure from the tenor of the remainder of the document.

Then there is the question of why it is even thought important to advocate that "employees (be enabled) to become owners of stock in the companies for which they work" (#248). After all, are not the workers in a firm, and all other citizens for that matter, perfectly free to use their savings for this purpose?[14]

It is interesting to ask why American employees have remained so unconvinced by the blandishments of Kelso and his followers, and have failed to purchase stock certificates to the degree desired by those who are urging this scheme on a reluctant work-force. In order to appreciate why this should be so, we might reflect on the benefits traditionally conferred by the employer on his employee.

Employee benefits

These are mainly twofold. First of all, the capitalist-employer advances his workforce the wherewithal to live until the final product is sold on the market. For no matter how short an interval is involved, the creation of a good or service always takes *time*, and in some cases the interval between the inception of an idea and the sale of the good can take decades. Were it not for the employer, and were the laborers organized in the form of workers cooperatives as advocated by the bishops, then it is they upon whom the burden of raising these monies would fall. It is only thanks to the past savings of the businessman (either their own, or borrowed funds) that there is a firm which can supply the capital and raw materials necessary for paid employment during their production process.

Secondly, it is the entrepreneur who bears the *risk* of the entire operation. The firm and all its employees might struggle mightily, and for many years, but in the kaleidic world in which we live there is simply no guarantee that when the product finally appears it will be able to sell for an amount that will compensate the workers for their efforts; it is even possible that, due to entirely unforseen circumstances (e.g., obsolescence, changing consumer tastes), the good will not be able to be sold at all. Were the firm organized under the principles of worker cooperative ownership, it is the laborers who would have to bear this risk.

In contrast, in the more traditional employer-employee firm, the owner of an unsold product cannot go back to the workers he has been paying all along and demand a refund of the wages he gave them on the ground that their product is now found to be unmarketable. The very idea is ludicrous. No, it is the firm which bears the risk. The employer is the "residual income claimant," which means that he and he alone keeps the monies from the sale of the final product after all factors have been paid off. But this holds true whether this residual income is positive (profits) or negative (losses).

Setting terms

If the employer bears the risks, and if it is due to his past scrimping that there is a business at all,[15] then simple justice would appear to demand that he be free to set any employment terms he wishes, with employees free, of course, to accept or reject them. Of course, the employer may not coerce anyone into working for him; but it would appear appropriate for him at least to be allowed to set the conditions upon which the labor contract would be determined, and then wait and see if he could attract a work-force on this basis.

What are we to make, then, of this view expressed by the bishops?

> ... a collaborative and mutually accountable model of industrial organization demands that workers not have to bear all the burdens of a dynamic economy in transition. Management and investors must also make their share of the sacrifices, especially, for example, when management is contemplating transferring capital to a potentially more productive or competitive location. The capital at the disposal of management represents to a significant degree the investment of the labor of those who have toiled in the company over the years, including currently employed workers. It is patently unjust to deny these workers any role in shaping the outcome of such difficult choices. As a minimum, workers have a right to be informed in advance when such decisions are under consideration, a right to negotiate with management about possible alternatives and a right to fair compensation and assistance with retraining and relocation expenses should these be necessary (#245).

This is highly problematic. To begin with, the capital presently at the disposal of management represents not at all the investment of its work-force. Assuming that the firm had not gone bankrupt and cheated its employees out of their wages, the company has been *paying* its laborers all along for their efforts. What remains from the final sale of the product after all factors, including labour, have been compensated belongs to the owners of the business concern, *not* to the workers. It is therefore, contrary to the claim made above, entirely just to deny workers any role whatsoever in shaping the outcome of such difficult choices.[16] If the workers want to take part in this sort of decision-making, let them follow the advice of Mr. Kelso and the bishops and invest some of their *own* hard-earned money in business enterprises; until they have done so, let them leave off their spurious claims for a role in corporate decision-making.

Plant closings

The same analysis holds true with regard to plant closings. Whether or not to open up a plant in the first place should be up to the sole discretion of the owners, and they and they alone should be able to determine whether, and on what conditions, the plant should be closed down.

In the bishops' view, however:

> the best medicine for the disease of plant closings is prevention. Prevention depends not only on sustained capital investment to enhance productivity through advanced technology, but also on the training and retraining of workers within the private sector .... In addition, in circumstances where plants are forced to shut down, management, labor unions and local communities must see to it that workers are not simply cast aside (#183).

For the bishops, then, plant closings are an entirely negative phenomenon. They are to be avoided if at all possible, and if not, their detrimental effects upon the employers are to be cushioned, at the expense of management.[17] But this is an improper understanding of the economics of plant closings. If no factories were ever shut down, no matter what kind of economic events occurred, several negative consequences would prevail. For one thing, inefficiency would increase, as the old plants were unable to as readily convert resources (land, labor, capital, raw material, etc.) into final products. For another, misallocation would ensue, as industrial capacity would not be as able to create the new kinds of goods now wanted. (Where are the hula hoop factories now?) Thirdly, U.S. plant and equipment would be rendered geographically inflexible by an anti plant-closing policy. Oil price changes, demographics, population migration all have implications for the optional location of factories and mills. But with plant closings hindered, these alterations cannot as easily take place. As well, if government enacts stronger and stronger legislation imposing all sorts of obligations on plant management in the event of a shut down, fewer such facilities will be opened up in the first place.

Richard B. McKenzie points out that the costs involved are by no means trivial, and can add up to as much as a billion dollars (over a three-year period) for a single firm (thus putting at extreme risk the jobs of its employees at its other plants, which, paradoxically, would have been safe, but for this policy).[18] As well, he calls attention to the fact that:

> To operate in a financially sound manner under such a law over the long run, a company must prepare for the eventual expenditure associated with closing: it can establish its own contingency fund or buy insurance against the risk that it must assume. Either way, the cost will be recovered from wages that would otherwise have been paid, or from higher prices charged consumers, in which case the purchasing power of workers' incomes is reduced. Owners of companies will be hurt by the legislation — no question about it — but that is not the point that needs emphasis. Workers will not escape paying for the benefits received under the restrictions.[19]

VI. SUBSIDIARITY

The last topic to be discussed under the heading of economic collaboration is that of subsidiarity. According to this doctrine, "social problems are best dealt with at the lowest level of society capable of dealing with them, with appeal to higher centralized authority only in case of necessity."[20] This part of traditional Catholic social teaching is relevant to our concerns, since according to the bishops, one of the guiding principles of economic collaboration ought to be subsidiarity.

This teaching is so important a part of Catholic doctrine that according to Michael Novak, "There are three fundamental principles of Catholic social thought: the dignity of the human person, the social nature of human life, and the principle of subsidiarity (decisions should be made by those closest to the realities involved)."[21]

Politics is supposed to make strange bedfellows, and religion must do so also, for the doctrine of subsidiarity is all but indistinguishable from views called, alternatively, "states' rights" (which was used for many years by reactionary forces in their attempt to stave off the civil rights revolution), and "local control" (which was the rallying cry of presumably "progressive" forces, in places such as Brooklyn's Ocean Hill-Brownsville, in their attempt to wrest control of schooling from the centralized New York City Board of Education).

No matter how widespread the support for subsidiarity under whatever rubric, the doctrine has several serious flaws.

First of all, on purely theological grounds, it would appear to fly in the face of yet another basic Catholic belief — that of papal supremacy. For the pope is located in the Vatican, which is in Italy. Because of the laws of geography, he will of necessity be located far away from the "realities involved" in many local social problems. To be sure, the doctrine can be saved at the formal level by the proviso that appeal can be made to "higher centralized authority" in cases of "necessity," but this only shows how weak a reed is subsidiarity — it tends to stretch at the first conflict with a competing doctrine, in this case that of the primacy of central authority.

Proximity

Secondly, there is the difficulty that in many cases mere geographical proximity to a given social problem may have little correlation with ability to solve it. In many cases, the locals may be too close to the matter to be able to come to grips with it; they may be in need of a fresh perspective, perhaps attainable only from an outsider. It is not for nothing that the "outside expert" is often called in to wrestle with a predicament which has baffled "those closest to the realities involved."

And a third point, perhaps most important of all, is that this doctrine is in conflict with rights, something the bishops are on record as supporting. For according to subsidiarity, an absentee landlord, or a stockholder located a great distance from the plant in question, would be far removed from the reality involved; hence, his wishes or solutions should be ignored, or at least given far less weight than those of the people close at hand. But the absentee landlord or stockholder may well have the *right* to determine how the problem shall be resolved. Subsidiarity, in ignoring this elemental canon of justice, is therefore seen as incompatible with the goal of erecting public policy on a moral base.

As well, were subsidiarity actually implemented, and absentee landlords, stockholders and other such capitalists disenfranchised of their respective property rights, this would sound the death-knell of all such modes of investment. As a result, it would be all but impossible to raise funds from "outsiders," for "local" projects. If those "closest to the realities involved" are to be granted the right to make the relevant decisions, they will end up having to do so with regard to projects financed from their own funds. They may be able to effectively expropriate investments made by people far away from the local scene when subsidiarity is first implemented, but as in the proverbial tale of the goose that laid the golden eggs, these monies will soon enough dry up.

Subsidiarity is also contrary to the bishops' espousal of Kelso-type schemes which call for worker investment in the firms which employ them. For under such arrangements, the hard-earned wages of the employees are put at risk — if ever they choose to move away, as they may well do at least with the advent of retirement. If so, then they will be considered as not "best able" to deal with any "local" problems which arise, and their interests, too, can be set aside by a policy which has little respect for private property rights.

Notes

1. See 15, pp. 6-7.
2. It is impossible to over-use this phrase. If President Reagan is remembered for nothing else, his place in history will be secure as a wordsmith extraordinaire.
3. Said Adam Smith of this process "By directing that industry in such manner as its produce may be of the greatest value, and he is in this, as in many other cases, led by an invisible hand to promote an end there was no part of his intention ... By pursuing his own interest he frequently promotes that of our society more effectually than when he really intends to promote it."
4. See 36, p. 338, #89.
5. See 24, p. 15.
6. See 36, #242, where the bishops call for "a new experiment in cooperation and collaboration."
7. Even the communist nations, in actual practice, allow for the private ownership of household goods. "Economic democracy," if carried to its logical conclusion, would not.
8. See 17, p. 22.
9. Paul Heyne characterizes a similar proposal as "a recipe for either chaos or tyranny," see 15, p. 9. John Langan notes that the participation urged by the bishops is "a very difficult thing to make real in an economy with the scale and the characteristics or our economy, and that's true for people who are a lot better off then the really poor" (see 19, p. 104). This is true as far as it goes, but it does not go far enough. Certainly it is "very difficult" for anyone to "participate" in the economy along the lines favored by the bishops, and that this applies to all people, rich or poor. But it is not a matter of mere "difficulty." Were such a scheme ever inaugurated, and seriously carried out, it would literally cripple the entire economy. No one could make any decision, no matter how minor, without inviting all other members of society to take part. The major drawback to socialism, according to some wags, is that it requires all too many committee meetings. This, too, is the problem with "participation." It would take so much time to implement, that there would be very little of an economy left for the "participants" to administer. Michael Novak underestimates the flaw in the doctrine of participation. In his view, participa-

tion would appear to be equivalent to full-time employment, for he objects to the doctrine on the ground that "a majority of the poor cannot participate fully in the economic system; because of their youth, old age, disabilities, illness or responsibilities for small children, some persons are inherently dependent upon others," (see 19, p. 113). But it is the bishops' view that participation is a right of all people, one which flows only from their membership in the human race; mere incapacity, as per Novak, would not, in their understanding, preclude anyone, able or not, from having the right to affect the economic decision-making which impacts on their lives. It is true that the bishops concede that "the level of participation in these different sectors of social life may legitimately be greater for some persons than for others" (#94), but this only means that they realize that some people must have more of an effect on economic decision-making than others. (Strictly speaking, this is a retreat from the doctrine of full and equal participation.) The bottom line is that all people, even the unemployable, must, in the opinion of BP, have some input into determining the pattern of the economy. State the bishops: "... there is a minimum level of access that must be made available for all"(#94), and "justice demands the establishment of minimum levels of participation by all persons in the life of the human community" (#92).

10. See Ludwig von Mises, Socialism; Friedrich A. Hayek; *Collective Economic Planning*.

11. The bishops are not the only ones to call strenuously for "balance." The Lay Letter, too, appeals for balance and compromise on numerous occasions, also without venturing deeply out into the intellectual waters upon which such a conclusion could be based. For example, the Lay Letter appeals for "balance" between government intervention into the economy, a free market system, and the institutions of moral and cultural life (family, church, press, universities) without outlining the basis upon which such a determination could be made, nor indicating the appropriate weights to be given to each (see 25, p. 11); it calls for a compromise between the Adam Smithian notion of a limited government night watchman state, and a managerial state along socialist lines (25, p. 30); it counsels "balance" between labor and management, again, without indicating the rights of each (25, p. 36).

There is an aphorism according to which "patriotism is the last refuge of the scoundrel." If we were to attempt a similar, but relevant saying, it might be the view that "balance is the last refuge of those who are ambivalent, or economically innocent, or unsure of their position." One of the benefits of the "golden mean," after all, is that if one takes this position on a number of issues, over the long haul, one is perhaps most likely to come closest to the truth. But as a substitute for analysis, in any one particular case, it is a recipe for disaster.

Would this call for balance extend to the issue of slavery? No one ever accused Lloyd Garrison of having a balanced perspective on this particular institution. He was clearly an extremist. But this hardly put him in the wrong. The war against the Nazis was also an extreme non-balanced response. Was it thereby rendered immoral? Is "extremism in defence of liberty," in the words of Barry Goldwater, now to be considered per se vice? Hardly. It all depends upon the specifics of the case in point. Thus, we are not entitled to deduce from only the fact that one policy is extreme, and the other "balanced," that the latter is preferable to the former on moral grounds. The case for an intermediate position between that of Karl Marx and that of Adam Smith will have to be argued on its own merits. It is simply not sufficient to note that both of these are extreme (true enough), and that therefore a point on the political economic spectrum achieved by adding them up and dividing by two would be preferable to either one.

12. See 36, p. 340. See also #s 114, 245, 248.

13. See Louis Kelso and P. Hetter, "Corporate Social Responsibility Without Corporate Suicide," *Challenge*, July/August 1973, pp. 52-57; for a critique of the Kelso doctrine, see Timothy P. Roth, "The Economics of Property Rights Transferal: The Case of ESOPs, GSOPs and CSOPs" in *Privitization Theory and Practice*, Michael A. Walker, ed. Vancouver: The Fraser Institute, 1980.

14. It might be salutary for business, and perhaps even for the preservation of the capitalist system, if employees were to make a special effort to purchase the goods and services created by the firms which employ them. But there is little reason to use scarce public policy resources to advocate this, since workers, and all other consumers, are perfectly free to do so in any case.

15. Of course, the owner of the firm need not himself save the money necessary to purchase the machines and raw materials — and pay salaries — until the final good can be sold. As an alternative, he can borrow the money from willing investors. But if he does so, this capital is still *his* responsibility. It is *his* business reputation, and hence future ability to borrow money, that is at risk if he cannot make good this debt.

16. This is entirely just, but it may not be entirely wise. That is to say, even though employees have no right to a voice in such decisions, and employers thus have no moral obligation to give it to them, it still may be the better part of valour to hear their opinions in any case, perhaps through such traditional employer-created institutions as the suggestion box.

17. The bishops call upon "labor unions and local communities" (#162) to pitch in as well, but this is somewhat disingenuous. For labor unions, in theory, are the organized embodiment of the workers themselves. Asking the labor unions to help out, for the bishops, is thus like asking the employees to help themselves. This, they would presumably do in any case, so the BP has placed no extra burden upon the organized workforce through this call. And, to a somewhat lesser degree, the same thing applies to the similar demand upon "local communities." Given the relative number of employees and employers involved in any likely plant shut-down in a local community, this, too, is almost akin to asking the workers to help themselves.

18. See his "The Case for Plant Closures," *Policy Review*, Vol. 15, Winter 1981, pp. 123-124.

19. *Ibid.*, see also Richard B. McKenzie, *Competing Visions: The Political Conflict over America's Economic Future*, Washington, D.C.: Cato, 1985.

20. See 16, p. 8.

21. See 30, p. B1.

CHAPTER 6

INTERNATIONAL ECONOMIC POLICY

The bishops begin this section with two truths which deserve to be highlighted. They start (#269) by indicating that national boundaries must take a back seat to economic policy requirements. (In #273, they refer to "the flaws in the traditional notion of national sovereignty.") This is a crucially important perspective from which to begin an analysis of international economics — particularly one which strives to mobilize moral, religious and philosophical underpinnings — because, at bottom, we are *all* children of God. All the world's peoples, from each and every corner of the globe, have rights; moreover, these rights are the equal of those of anyone else, no matter which sovereign nation state now claims their allegiance. But economic nationalism, the doctrine that makes invidious distinctions among human beings on the basis of differential citizenship, is clearly at odds with these principles.[1]

The second truth deserving of emphasis is the focus they place on "the scandal of the shocking inequality between the rich and the poor" (#270). The inequality of wealth and income between rich and poor countries is shockingly great,[2] and it is no less than an outrage that such should be the case.

Unhappily, however, BP sees an alleviation of this situation mainly in terms of an "intensifying imperative of distributive justice in a world sharply divided between rich and poor"(#270). This is problematic since, as we have seen above, so-called distributive justice is not really justice, but rather forced transfers of wealth (i.e., theft) on such a massive scale that the moral realities remain all but hidden. A second difficulty is that as a matter of strict logic there are not one but two ways to erase an income gap between rich and poor. One, which the bishops clearly have in mind, is to raise the wealth of the poor toward the level attained by the rich giving to the former what was taken by the latter; but another way is to *lower* the well being of the rich until it approaches that presently suffered by the poor. It shall be the contention of the present critique that although the bishops intend to strengthen the poor by weakening the rich, if the public policies they recommend were put into place, they would only weaken the rich. And worse. For not only would these methods impoverish the industrialized and economically developed West, they would actually decrease the economic status of people living in the underdeveloped countries of the Third World, paradoxical as that appears at first glance.

A scandal

A third drawback to the "scandal hypothesis," at least the version presented in BP, is that the finger of blame is pointing in the wrong direction. It is indeed a "scandal" that "in a $12 trillion world economy" that of the U.S. "alone accounts for more than a fourth"(#276). But the scandal is not that Americans have been so productive, well organized and resourceful — it is that the rest of the world has been, relatively, so slothful and disorganized. This, of course, is due in no small measure to the fact that the U.S. retains at least a small measure of the economic freedom advocated by Adam Smith, while much of the rest of the world, particularly the underdeveloped countries, struggles under virtually its polar opposite: marxist dictatorships of the "proletariat."

The bishops' are not without a defense against this charge. In their view, the rich nations are rich and the poor ones poor not because of differing political-economic ideologies, but rather due to exploitation: "... the relationship between developing countries and industrialized countries resembles the interdependence, respectively, of horse and rider" (#277).[3] Indeed, virtually the entire section of the BP dealing with international economic relationships (#s 268-319) may be viewed as a parading of the case that the advanced nations owe their wealth to expropriation of the underdeveloped countries of the Third World. Let us consider these arguments in detail.

I. AGRARIAN DUALISM

The first heading under which the bishops make their case is trade, and they begin with what has been called the argument of agrarian dualism. This point is made in #275:

> Thousands of peasants in Colombia have been driven from their farms
> to marginal lands or to urban slums to make way for the producers

of export crops, like cut flowers for the North American market; similarly, peasants in Northeast Brazil were displaced in favor of producers of soybeans to feed the cattle of Europe and Asia.

As well, in #311, they state "producing cash crops for export instead of food crops needed for local consumption" is seen as an instance of one of the many "present inequities in a developing country."

This argument, it must readily be admitted, has a certain surface plausibility. If people are going hungry, it is irresponsible to produce cut flowers or soybean cattle-feed. Human beings, after all, cannot eat such items. But a moment's reflection will indicate that things are not that simple; could not be that simple. For if they were, it would not only pay for hungry farmers to grow food staples — it would pay for everyone else in society to follow this path as well. If cut flowers cannot directly feed the hungry, even less so can steel, automobiles, books, piano lessons, or taxi cab services. Should the purveyors of these goods — and for that matter, all other non agricultural employees — leave off their tasks, and hie back to the farms? Hardly. If they did, paradoxically, we would eventually have less food, not more, as our entire economy unravelled. And yet this is the policy prescription implied by agrarian dualism.

The key word, here, is "directly." Of course people cannot directly produce foodstuffs by pursuing these other occupations. But they can do so indirectly, that is, by first manufacturing these other items, and then trading them for food. Moreover, this is a more efficient method of producing edibles, at least for a large complex modern society. If a music teacher can obtain more food by first giving piano lessons and then trading in the proceeds for food, than by directly producing meals out of the ground herself, then so can many other people, even an entire nation. In like manner, one of Holland's prime exports is tulips; and Holland is hardly a starving country. Unfortunately, were the advice of BP followed, and crops changed from a non-food to a food orientation, the lot of peoples in these Third World countries would be reduced in terms of ability to eat well. The bishops' claim that the production of cut flowers or other non-food items is part and parcel of the economic exploitation of underdeveloped countries thus cannot be sustained. Typical of the doctrine called agrarian dualism is the following statement: "Drought stricken African nations are caught in a 'debt trap' that forces them to grow exotic foods to earn foreign currency while their own citizens starve. A glaring example is the fact that Ethiopia is sending exports of watermelons to the United Kingdom while thousands of Ethiopians are dying of starvation.[4]

Such critiques constitute an attack on no less a main pillar of economics than the doctrine of comparative advantage. The Western democracies owe their present great wealth to the division of labor, specialization, and trade — the very institutions now being criticized by the bishops. Perhaps these concepts can best be explained in contrast to their polar opposite, self-sufficiency. Under a regime of self-sufficiency, each person would produce all that he needed. But it is easy to see that we would starve to death under such conditions because no one knows how to do all the things that are required to sustain life. We in North America are as wealthy as we are because we can specialize. One person can build houses another can grow potatoes, and yet a third can give music lessons. Productivity rises, as we each master our trades. But no one can survive on only houses, or bread, or music lessons. So trade with each other is crucial. The U.S. can produce maple syrup, Costa Rica can grow bananas, and we can trade, and each can benefit. If we could not trade, and we had to be self-sufficient, this earth that can now support five billion people, could do so for far fewer. So trade, specialization and a division of labor are necessary for the very lives of most of this earth's inhabitants.

Despite claims to the contrary, it may well pay for Ethiopia to continue producing watermelons, etc. In a market society, paradoxically, Ethiopians can attain more staple food by producing watermelons or tulips, or strawberries for the tables of the rich than they can by producing the staple foods directly for themselves. In like manner, philosophers, typists, doctors, can buy more cars by tending to their own businesses than by making cars themselves. The attorney can create more yachts by sticking to his profession than by making the boats himself; the baker can have more watermelon by specializing in cookie and bun production than by part-time farming. So, it is senseless to say that it does not pay the Third World countries to produce things they don't use themselves, that it is exploitative to trade in such a manner. And yet, that is the theory that cash crops for foreign export are economically harmful.

Consider another version of this sentiment: "Many countries should strike a better balance between food crops and cash crops raised for export. Chad recently reaped a bumper cotton harvest, but its people are dying for want of home grown food."[5] Conceivably, it was a mistake to grow the cotton. This would not be a great surprise because the government of Chad relies on central planning. Under these conditions, the individual farmer cannot pick and choose the best crop. Nor is there any profit and loss system which rewards the efficient farmer and penalizes the inefficient. But suppose that there were private entrepreneurs in Chad, and that they decided, in effect, that planting cotton was the best and most efficient means of feeding themselves; i.e. that they were of the opinion that they could get more wheat, etc., by producing cotton and trading it for wheat, than they could get by producing the wheat in the first place. If correct, they would have more wheat, not less. It is naive in the extreme to suppose that cotton is a poor crop to plant if you want to feed yourself, just because you can't eat it.

But perhaps the situation in some Third World countries is far different. Here, it may be supposed, the tulips, cotton, watermelon were grown not because the farmers chose that crop, but because a coercive multinational corporation has previously stolen the land from the peasants. Now, as the landowner, the multinational corporation decides to plant tulips on its ill-gotten lands.

The objection, however, is ill-conceived as a bulwark of the agrarian dualism doctrine. For, suppose that justice prevails and the evil multinational corporation is made to disgorge its stolen lands, and return them to the peasants from whom they were taken. What will the peasants now plant? Presumably tulips, not wheat or rice that can be directly consumed. If it was economic for the thieving multinational corporation to plant tulips, it would be equally so for peasants to do the same! They, too, will choose tulips.

Terms of trade

The next attempt on the part of the bishops to document Third World exploitation has to do with the terms of trade. In their view:

> Any realistic appraisal of the role of developing countries in the world economy suggests that their importance will continue to grow and that for the foreseeable future they will import more than they export. At the same time, when we see the disadvantageous terms of trade under which the developing countries operate (their imports cost them far more than their exports can earn), we come to the same conclusion that prompted Pope Paul VI to describe international trade as the testing ground of social justice for the developing countries (#296).[6]

But this will not do. Only a strong mercantilist[7] influence would impel the bishops to make such a statement. If imports cost more in total than can be earned by exports, the underdeveloped nations would do well to adopt an obvious change in policy: cut back on purchases until they are within their budget limitations.

As a matter of fact, the bishops' description of disadvantageous terms of trade sounds all too reminiscent of the typical family's budget practices in the last few weeks before Christmas: lots of additional spending, only the usual income, and as a result, increased debt. Are we then to conclude that the terms of trade faced by the family somehow mysteriously deteriorate right before each Christmas? Hardly.

The usual way to claim deterioration in the terms of trade is not in terms of total sales or income (exports) in comparison with total purchases (imports), but rather on the basis of prices which one pays as a consumer (importer) relative to the prices which one receives in payment for one's product (exports). Let us consider the 'declining terms of trade' argument in more detail. Commodity price ratios have been falling, it is alleged by the bishops. This is another explanation put forth to try to account for starvation in the Third World. But the West does not control the terms of trade. If it did, how is it that the terms of trade ever rose for primary produce? The terms of trade for primary products as against manufactured goods continually fluctuate. If the West controls it, why would it ever rise? So that argument does not hold. The terms of trade, or the relative prices of agricultural commodities compared to manufactured, is a function of numerous suppliers and demanders all over the world.

Furthermore, it is better to have some terms of trade than none. It is simply invalid to reason that since declining terms of trade for agricultural and tropical products can harm the Third World, we should have no terms of trade at all, i.e. a cessation of trade. This view would lead to a cut in the commercial ties between the Third World and the West. But trade benefits both parties — at whatever terms of trade. As we have seen, an extra option must enrich all parties; otherwise they are each free to reject it. Moreover, if the terms of trade against primary products are so bad, how is it that producers of primary products in North America and Western Europe are not starving? How is it that the agricultural sectors in the advanced Western countries are not famine-ridden? Obviously, the supposedly "poor" terms of trade have not succeeded in creating desolation in the prairies: therefore, they could not create such conditions in the underdeveloped world. We have to seek elsewhere for an explanation.[8]

Free trade

If the bishops are clear, at least in their own minds, that agrarian dualism and deteriorating terms of trade are instances of exploitation of the impoverished nations of the world by Western capitalism, their attitude toward the doctrine of full and free trade between all countries in this regard is more complex. On the one hand, they register a welcome receptivity toward this element of laissez-faire. State the bishops, "within a frame of reference characterized by the 'preferential option for the poor,' we lean toward an open trading system" (BP, p.341).

But on the other hand, they hem in their otherwise magnificent call for free trade with such a welter of restrictions, caveats, warnings, cautions and admonitions that the purity of their position is hopelessly compromised. For example, they "require a trading system that is both free and *fair*" (emphasis added), (BP, p. 341); in #298, the bishops also call for "fair" trade.[9]

Fair trade

The idea behind "fair" trade is that all participants should be able to "play ball" on a level playing field.[10] That is to say, no one should be given an advantage — or, even more important, be made to suffer a disadvantage. According to this doctrine, if the Ruritanian government gives its widget industry a subsidy, which enables it to undersell American producers, then the domestic industry should be able to apply for an offsetting tariff, which would once again allow them to compete on a "fair" basis with their foreign counterparts.

Like all economic fallacies which have attracted numerous followers, this one, too, has a certain superficial credibility. We would certainly never hold an Olympic competition where some entrants were forced to carry 50 pound weights on their backs, and others not; or some allowed to run downhill, while others were forced to run uphill.

But this analogy between sports and commerce is invalid. Athletics is an enterprise which can be won by only one party. In trade, both participants can gain. Each gains the difference (in his own evaluation or estimation) between what he must give up (the leisure for an employee, a good for a person enjoyed in barter, a product for a retailer)[11] and what he receives in return (the employee's wages, another item for the barterer, a money payment for the retailer). Unless what is given up is worth less to the economic actor than what is received, he will not agree to engage in the trade in the first place.[12]

Consider for a moment the West German reparations made to the state of Israel. These of course were made in terms of money, so the case is, strictly speaking, irrelevant to our present concerns. But let us suppose that these payments were in the form of Volkswagens instead. If they were, then we would have an extreme case of an uneven playing field, or "unfair" trade. For under these circumstances, it would be well nigh impossible to set up any kind of automobile manufacturing industry in Israel. It simply would not pay for an Israeli to set up such an operation. How could he compete with hordes of rushing Volkswagens which were not only subsidized slightly (thus making a cheap price feasible) but which were subsidized so heavily that they could be had by the Israeli consumer virtually for free?

Perhaps it is "unfair" that under such a scenario an Israeli auto industry would be unfeasible, but any attempt to do "right" by these as yet non-existent firms — under the principle of "fairness" — would certainly redound to the detriment of the consumer in the Holy Land. "Fairness," in other words, is in this context diametrically opposed to the well-being of the consumer. Since this is what economic prosperity is all about — consumer satisfaction — the bishop's concern with "fairness" is thus at odds with their championship of economic development, and ultimately with the preferential option for the poor — the material improvement in the lives of the impoverished.[13]

Balancing rights

Another BP caveat with regard to free trade arises in the context of the "adverse impact" this policy may have on the domestic "workers and their families" of a country adopting this policy. Only if these effects are "cushioned," should the U.S. adopt it, we are told (#297). This conflict in rights is also expressed by the bishops as follows: "For the U.S., trade also puts increasing stress on the link between foreign policy and domestic politics: Claims of injustice from developing countries denied market access are countered by claims of injustice in the domestic economy where jobs are threatened" (#299).[14]

There are two ways of looking at matters of this sort. The one adopted by the bishops is that there is only so much work to be done on this earth; if foreigners do more of it — by succeeding in exporting more goods to the U.S. — then there will be less left for Americans to do. Under this philosophy, every mechanical innovation, every increase in international trade, every scientific advance, must be looked upon suspiciously, lest it "steal" a precious job from a needy domestic worker.

The alternative, an economic approach, is that there is simply no limit to the amount of work that needs to be done. Or more strictly, the only upper bound to further employment is man's desire for additional goods. As long as people want more than they have — yachts, spaceships, violin lessons, cancer cures, whatever — their demands will create sufficient additional jobs so that everyone who wants one may obtain one.[15] In this vision, we need not fear the inroads of exports from abroad. If foreigners sell more goods to U.S. citizens, what will they do with the dollars they receive? If they spend them in America, this will create jobs in industries producing the items desired by the peoples from other countries. If they use these dollars in other nations, they will eventually come back to U.S. shores with the same effect. But suppose these dollars never come back to their country of origin and continually circulate abroad (i.e., the eurodollar market). Or, more dramatically, that the people who originally sell Americans their goods stuff the dollars they receive in exchange under their mattresses, or even burn them. Will such practices be able to deal a death blow to U.S. employment? It would appear so, for in this case there would be no additional jobs created in the industries servicing U.S. trading partners, to compensate for the ones lost due to additional imports.

A mirage

But this is a mirage. For the scenario just described is equivalent to one in which people from abroad give gifts to Americans.[16] In such a situation, American labor would be freed up from manufacturing things hitherto created domestically.[17] Now, they would be able to create additional goods and services, which could not otherwise have been produced when they were busy manufacturing the things the foreigners now give to the Americans, for free.

If one compares the American economy of 1980 with that of, say, 1880, this is exactly what happened! Only instead of foreigners bringing gifts of great swatches of their GNPs to the U.S., it is as if time itself (i.e., innovation, scientific advancement) has brought additional bounty. A century ago,[18] the total labor force was 14,745,000. As of the last census, this figure had risen to 108,544,000. In 1880, 48.3 percent of the labor force was on the farm; as of 1980, the equivalent figure is only 3.4 percent. Why don't we have an unemployment rate of one minus the other, or 44.9 percent? Where did all the additional non-agricultural positions come from? This is impossible to answer under the there-is-only-so-much-work-to-be-done-and-if-foreigners-do-more-we'll-have-less-for-ourselves hypothesis. But when looked upon from the economic perspective the question is easily answered: the new jobs are the manifestations of goods and services desired by people in 1980 that would have been impossible to produce under the technology of 1880.

In 2080, hopefully, there will be many more jobs than at present. Whole industries will be all but wiped out (just as agricultural employment has been decimated over the past 100 years). Robots, perhaps, will be making things like automobiles, textiles, shoes, T.V. sets, under the most minimal of human supervision. Will we have an unemployment rate of 44.9 percent? Not unless the laws of economics are repealed. Instead, precious human labor that had to be expended on these items given the backward technology of 1980 will be released — and thus enabled to do the things, whatever they are, that our great grandchildren will require for an appropriate standard of living, 2080-style.

So we see that there is no need to "balance" the rights of foreigners to export their merchandise to the U.S., against the right of the domestic labor force to employment. A policy of full free trade can accommodate both.

The cushion

Let us now address the call in the BP for the U.S. to "adopt adequate programs to cushion the possible adverse impact of freer trade on their own workers and families" (#297).

This, too, is incompatible with the principle of the preferential option of the poor. For who is it that is likely to need "cushioning" from the winds of international competition? Let us be exhaustive, and consider all the candidates. First of all, there are of course the capitalists. They made the investment; if it succeeds, they will profit. If it fails, it is they and they alone who should bear the losses. Unfortunately for the cause of justice, they are the ones who typically receive the lion's share of "cushioning." But the bishops certainly do not ask for government bailouts in their behalf.

Next, there are the workers. But the workers, too, are capitalists of a sort. That is to say, they have made investments in themselves, in their skills, training and talents. This is sometimes called "human capital" in the fevered jargon of the economist.[19] Just as in the case of physical capital, human capital admits of degrees. We can, at the very least, distinguish between those who have more, and those who have less. The former are the highly skilled; they are often likely to be unionized; if anyone does not fit into the category of the poor, for whom we are to exercise a "preferential option," it is they. The latter, in contrast, are poorly skilled. They likely occupy the lowest paying dead-end jobs and are not usually to be found in the ranks of organized labor. Of all those who actually have jobs, they are the prime example of people to whom the appellation "preferential option for the poor" applies.

But who is it that typically loses out from imports? Who is it that needs cushioning the least, but who, because of our political process, is most likely to receive it? The answer to all these questions is the highly skilled, not those who can boast of only moderate investments in their human capital.

Suppose cheap Japanese steel, or autos, or inexpensive Southeast Asian textiles and footwear come flooding into the U.S. under a regime of free trade, and the employees in these industries are thus forced to make the adjustments, by accepting jobs in other industries.[20] Who will lose out to a greater degree: the relatively unskilled person who used to sweep the floors of an auto or sweater plant, and can find similar employment elsewhere? Or the highly skilled machinist, or the foreman with 15 years of experience in a steel mill, whose training is not readily transferable to a new enterprise? Obviously, the latter. Moreover, in the ordinary course of events, it is the organized and skilled workers who are likely to pack the political clout to obtain the "cushioning." When the bishops add their powerful voices to those calling for further subsidies for workers forced to relocate due to rising foreign imports, they only exacerbate the injustice. The recipients of the "cushioning" are likely to be relatively wealthy and prosperous members of the middle class. These (human) capitalists are no more worthy of subsidies at general taxpayer expense than are the owners of the import-competing mills and factories the BP wisely ignored in their quest for more subsidies.

II. DEBT

The bishops begin their analysis of the debt situation afflicting the poorer countries of the world as follows:

> As a result of austerity measures adopted in Bolivia to obtain an International Monetary Fund loan, the price of the daily bread of the poor was doubled overnight. Kerosene, the fuel of the poor for light and cooking, went up 300 percent. Public transportation skyrocketed from 40 percent to 100 percent (sic) (#275).

But are these circumstances really the fault of the IMF, as implied by the bishops? Can we not probe any deeper, to discern the true villain of the piece? The problem with blaming the IMF is that this is like criticizing the bullet for killing the victim — rather than the murderer who unleashed it. To be sure, in some superficial sense the IMF may be considered the proximate cause of the Bolivian difficulties. But in a more deep and basic sense, the role played by the IMF is merely one of creditor; it is the Bolivian government that is the spendthrift debtor, now called upon to make good on its improvident borrowing.

In #s 303-306 the bishops see the debtor countries of South America, and especially the even poorer ones in Africa, almost as the aggrieved parties in the debt controversy, while they in effect look upon the creditor nations in North America and Western Europe as improperly grasping and impatient. But as a matter of justice, the money which is being discussed in this regard is the property of the lenders. If it is not repaid, it is they who will undergo a loss akin to the one suffered by the holdup victim at the hands of the gunman.

Yet this is exactly the course urged by the bishops upon the international creditors. That they "lengthen the payment period," and better yet allow for "some measure of forgiveness"(#305). Apart from being unjust, if followed, this advice would negatively impact the poor in the future.

For imagine the scenario a decade or two ahead, if the "moral" suasion urged by the bishops takes place now, and these debts are forgiven. Who would then have incentive to lend money to impoverished nations, with the spectre of "forgiveness" being urged when these new debts fall due? If loans were made in such an atmosphere, they would be ever so much more strict, than if no bout of "forgiveness" takes place now. Stricter controls on collateral would be insisted upon, higher interest rates would be negotiated, etc., so as to compensate the new lenders for the increased risk they must now bear when lending to the poor. Worse, such credit might be refused outright.

III. FOREIGN AID

Before beginning our analysis of the bishops' treatment of foreign aid, we must object to the very term itself. "Foreign aid" is biased and tendentious. By labelling the phenomenon in this manner we become pre-disposed to accept the so far unproven claim that it works; that is, that government-to-government transfers of funds[21] are actually of benefit to the poor nations of the world, particularly to their most impoverished citizens.[22] The bishops appear quite given to this predisposition. They insist, quite correctly and quite emphatically, that "the need for assistance to the developing (sic) world is undeniable" (#307). But from this undeniable premise alone they deduce that government-to-government transfers of funds shall be able to accomplish this task. They never once question[23] whether this is means toward this goal — or toward its very opposite.

The gist of the bishops' view on this matter may be summarized in this way:

> The U.S. should increase its commitment to foreign aid, both in quality and quantity. Though still the largest single donor, our nation lags behind most other industrial nations in the relative amount of aid we provide to the Third World" (BP, p.341). "We are also shocked and ashamed that the United States, the "inventor" of foreign aid, is now almost at the bottom of the list of 17 industrialized Organization for Economic Cooperation and Development countries in the percentage of gross national product devoted to concessional foreign assistance (grants and low-interest, long term loans) (#291).

Since nowhere in the BP is any consideration given to the hypothesis that foreign "aid" may prove detrimental to its intended beneficiaries,[24] we shall have to develop this case without much reference to that document.[25]

First of all foreign "aid" does not go directly to the impoverished people of the recipient countries, it goes to their rulers. At least in theory, these monies are given to Third World government to be spent on their subjects, and this is the assumption maintained by advocates of this system. But in point of fact, the funds increase the powers of the rulers, and ironically enable them to carry out the policies which are in large part responsible for the plight of their subjects in the first place.

According to Bauer and Yamey:

> The money sent via the direct method does not go to the pitiable figures whose photographs we see in the campaigns of the aid lobbies. It goes to their governments — that is, their rulers. All too often it is these very rulers who are responsible for the gruesome conditions depicted in aid publicity. Foreign aid enables them to go on pursuing policies harmful or even utterly destructive to the population at large. A depressing yet incomplete list includes: maltreatment and expulsion of productive minorities; suppression of trade in farm produce, simple implements, and consumer goods; state monopoly of import and export; large-scale underpayment of farmers; forced collectivization and coercive removal of people from their homes; wholesale confiscation for property; restriction on the inflow of badly needed skills, enterprise, and capital.[26]

As well, foreign "aid" sets up all sorts of counter-productive incentives. Just as we learned in the case of domestic welfare systems, when people are subsidized on the basis of poverty, it becomes in their interest, paradoxically, to be poor.

Bauer and Yamey tell us:

> To support rulers on the basis of the poverty of their subjects not only enables the rulers to pursue extremely damaging and even inhuman policies; it positively rewards them for doing so. Thus, per-capita incomes are reduced if a government restricts, persecutes, or expels its most productive people, often but not only ethnic minorities-Asians and Europeans in East Africa or Chinese in Southeast Asia; or if a government restricts the employment opportunities of women in the name of Islamic orthodoxy; or if it cripples or destroys the exchange economy. As incomes in the country are now lower, such governments can then qualify for more aid.[17]

Politicization

But foreign "aid" has yet another negative impact: it politicizes the people of the recipient country. Instead of embracing careers in private business, retailing, farming or manufacturing, the most intelligent and ambitious young people enter the civil service — in order to take advantage of the incoming "aid" funds. This tends to eviscerate the market sector, the engine of growth for the entire economy.

Moreover, the money influx tends to destabilize the society, and even create, or exacerbate civil strife. Under a system of laissez-faire, the system under which today's developed countries (e.g., U.S., U.K.) threw off the shackles of economic backwardness, it is a matter of supreme indifference who runs the ship of state. Government is so limited and narrowly prescribed that it rarely touches the people in their everyday lives.

But under a regime of central planning made possible by foreign "aid," it is a matter of extreme importance who is in control. Nay, it is no less than a matter of life and death, especially in countries with a history of tribal warfare. In such circumstances, it should be no surprise that foreign "aid" leads to strife, which in time decimates the economy and ruins any chance of growth.

In the view of Bauer and Yamey:

> While official aid represents a relatively small proportion of total government expenditures in Western countries (and therefore a yet smaller proportion of GNP), it is nevertheless substantial relative to government revenues and export earnings of recipient Third World countries, and often even exceeds them. The inflow of aid therefore much expands the resources and the power of governments. It reinforces and extends the politicization of life in the Third World. It increases the stakes — both gains and losses — in the struggle for political power, provokes or exacerbates anxiety and tension, particularly in the multiracial and multicultural societies of many Third World countries.
>
> The strains and tensions provoked by politicization often erupt into armed conflict even in countries where, in the past, different communities have lived together peaceably for generations — for instance in the Philippines, Malaysia, Indonesia, Burma, Sri Lanka, Chad, Uganda, and Nigeria. Politicization of life, reinforced by foreign aid, help to unleash the forces behind the recurrent or persistent civil wars in these countries. Among other effects, these sequences necessarily divert energy and resources from economic activity to political life. The poorest, especially the rural poor, are harmed most.

The misery in Ethiopia has been brought to the notice of many millions of people in the West. But not many have been told that the Marxist-Leninist government there has regularly received much Western aid, mostly from multilateral sources, with an appreciable U.S. and British content. This totaled about $1 billion over the five years 1978-82. Throughout this period, the government pursued most of the damaging and destructive policies we have listed above, including persecution of productive groups, coercive collectivization of agriculture, large-scale confiscation of property, and underpayment of farmers by state buying agencies. Western aid continued nevertheless.

What has happened to all this money? Obviously very little of it has gone to the poorest. Some of it has presumably helped the government to fight its several civil wars, and to finance the extravagant Organization of African Unity with headquarters in Addis Ababa.[28]

Then there is the view that foreign "aid" is needed to build economic structure (#307) or "infrastructure" (#310). This seems predicated on the idea that since the economics of Western Europe and Japan have a large infrastructure (public harbors, dams, highways, schools, etc.), this too is the way out of the morass for the underdeveloped countries of the Third World.

The problem, however, is that this wet-sidewalks-cause-rain theory is almost the complete reversal of the true cause effect relationship. These public sector initiatives do not cause economic growth; rather, they are only made possible by previous economic development.

Melvyn B. Krause comments in this regard on the

> productive private agriculture and small-to medium-size manufacturing businesses in the private sector having been ruined in order that the less-developed country could have highways when most of its citizens could not afford cars, telephone facilities when there was no business to transact over the telephones, modern office buildings to house useless bureaucrats, public monuments to the follies of the rulers who put them up, and schools that trained people for jobs that could not possibly exist without a prosperous private sector.[29]

IV. THE MULTINATIONAL CORPORATION

The bishops lead off their attack on the multinational corporation (MNC) with the observation that their power "to plan, operate, and communicate across national borders further increases the difficulty governments have in formulating effective and equitable trade policies" (#299). But this formulation assumes that governments can produce effective and equitable trade policies, while private enterprise cannot. No reasons, however, are given for this contention; in point of fact, the very opposite is much more nearly correct. For reasons discussed above, the political process is too blunt an instrument, its checks and balances a too infrequently occurring phenomenon, its information-communications system too arterio-sclerotic, to create an economic plan that is anything but inept. Given this difficulty, it is a matter to be welcomed, not regretted, that there is another institution, the MNC, which is able to evade the fumbling and interfering hand of government.

Elsewhere, in its discussion of foreign private investment (#s 310-313), the BP seems to almost welcome large infusions of funds to the "developing" countries, even if their main conduit is the MNC. However, this affirmation is so hemmed in with qualifications, that it is fair to say that the bishops are highly suspicious of any help from this quarter.

For example, the church leaders would accept a multination initiative "provided that it is consistent with the host country's goals, and that its benefits are equitably distributed" (#310). Thus, at one fell swoop the bishops practically dismiss the MNC as a positive economic actor in the drama of world hunger. If we take their words literally (and how else are we to consider the BP?) multinational investment would have to cease, forthwith. For MNC goals are completely at odds with those of the typical Third World dictator who is busily grinding down his subjects into abject poverty. The aim of all business concerns is to make profits. And they accomplish this by providing better offers[30] than their competitors to consumers, supplies, employees, etc., thus enriching all sectors of the economy, if they are successful.

In contrast, the chief aim of the typical dictator is to stay in power and enrich himself. He does this by killing his competitors, subduing and cowing his populace, and by pursuing economic policies which impoverish his country — the better to qualify for additional infusions of foreign "aid" from guilt-ridden Western governments, so as to be able to purchase still more monuments, machine guns and Mercedes.

Equity

If it would be disaster to impose the "host country's goals" on the MNC, so would it be to insist that the firm "equitably distribute"[31] its investment benefits. For it is only by the greatest of coincidences that the bishops' visions of equity would be congruent with the criteria of profit maximization. Instead of allocating investment on the principle of "equity,"[32] the MNC does so on the basis of productivity, reliability and other criteria which it expects will enhance profits. Insisting that investments be made, say, in backward unproductive interior regions, far from transport, because a factory is more "needed" there, is practically guaranteed to ensure that no business investment at all shall be forthcoming.

The bishops demand of such investment "Appropriateness should be determined jointly by the corporation and the responsible persons in the host country" (#311).[33] What if there *are* no "responsible persons" in the government of the host country? Should the people be made to suffer because of this tenet of the BP?[34]

Dependency

The next proviso insisted upon by the bishops is that MNC "investment in the developing countries (not) create or perpetuate dependency" (#311). But this is indeed strange. If there is any dependency created by international flows of funds, it is not through private business investment but rather from foreign "aid." For in the latter case, not the former, there are no profit and loss restrictions. Donor country governments have a free hand, relative to corporate boards. They are disbursing tax dollars, and hardly need earn a profit on them. They are accountable to electorates only infrequently, and it is the rare political campaign that turns on foreign "aid" alone. When is the last time a North American or Western European government fell on account of foreign "aid?" Yet, the International Monetary Fund and numerous other multinational government agencies are continually dictating economic policy to Third World governments.[35] Further, there is the threat of nationalization hanging over the MNC like a sword of Damocles. Private, not public agencies, are liable to be victimized by and to suffer from this process.[36]

When the factors are taken into account, it may be clear that the host government is dependent on donor countries, but it is no less clear that the MNC is dependent on the host country, once its factory has been put into place. Thus the bishops' fear of dependency creation should be redirected in behalf of international commercial ventures, where it is needed, and away from the Third World nations, where it is not.[37]

Exploiting workers

The bishops also insist that "Foreign private investment, attracted by low wage rates, can cut jobs in the home country and prolong the exploitation of workers in the host country" (#311).

However, it is very difficult for international (or any other) corporations to take advantage of low wage laborers. A business firm can only offer a wage above, below, or equal to the one prevailing before it came upon the scene. If the offered wage is higher, the worker must gain; if below, he need not accept employment; if the same, his condition is unchanged. It is hard to see, then, how the labor force of the undeveloped country can be exploited. Far from exploiting undeveloped countries, international firms have done more than anyone else, including perhaps all the world's welfare organizations put together, to drag them forward into the 20th century. Indeed, the main complaint heard from the developing world is that they receive too little multinational investment, not too much.

Nor are the U.S. companies motivated mainly by a search for cheap labor in their foreign hiring practices. The most oft-mentioned reasons for foreign investment are savings on transportation costs, proximity to raw materials and markets, avoidance of quotas, tariffs, and excessive taxation, and procurement of foreign skills and technology.

But even if foreign investment in low-wage areas were to occur on a massive scale, new employment would arise in the U.S. to take the place of the work farmed out. The reasons for the still unacceptably high unemployment rate in the U.S. are many and complex, but they do not include the hiring of cheap foreign labour. The proof? If foreign labor is truly cheaper than domestic, even when productivity and all other economic differentials are taken into account, then if a U.S. corporation were to fire some of its workers at home in order to hire cheaper ones abroad, costs will have to decrease. In turn, prices to the consumer will fall, output expand and profits rise. Any of these consequences — and certainly the combination of all three — will create jobs in the home country.

Consider a decrease in the final price of the good. Consumers in the U.S. who would have been willing to buy the product at the old price now have extra money in their pockets. Some of this will be saved, creating jobs in construction, basic industries, and investment, depending on how the money is loaned out by the banks. Some of it will be spent in this country for unrelated goods, creating new job opportunities in other fields.

And some of the money will be spent to buy more of the same good. This, along with the extra purchases by people who had not bought any at the old, higher price, will ensure the expansion of output. But more output requires more workers.

The higher profits will be distributed, in part, to the stockholders, increasing their purchasing power. This spending will create jobs for those displaced by foreign labor. Non-distributed profits will be retained by the corporation for internal expansion. This, too, will create employment opportunities for American workers.

The spending that is done abroad will not immediately help domestic employment. But eventually, when the foreigners use their earnings, some of the money will flow back to the U.S. and create export jobs.

Although it is impossible to pinpoint exactly where the new jobs will come from — new consumer spending, product expansion, profits, increased international trade — we can, with perfect certainty, conclude that they will come. For the number of jobs that need to be done is not finite and fixed for all time. A job is the manifestation of an unmet consumer desire. As long as people want more than they have, there will be work to be done, and opportunities for employment. This, as we have seen, is the only possible explanation of the fact that over 50 percent of our present jobs did not exist 100 years ago! Thus there is no reason to fear the employment of low-paid foreign labor. Americans, along with these people, can only gain from cooperation, an international division of labor, and trade.

The U.N.

The last point we shall consider under the rubric of international economic relations shall be the bishops' call for greater U.N. and multinational agency involvement. In #293 the BP takes the U.S. government to task for failure to sign the International Law of the Seas Treaty and the U.N. infant-formula resolution. In #312 the bishops express themselves as "particularly encouraged by the efforts of the United Nations to develop a code of conduct for foreign private investment that encourages both development and the equitable distribution of the benefits investment brings to the developing country. We urge the United States to support these efforts." Let us consider each in turn.

With regard to the Law of the Seas Treaty, its main effect would be to consign aquatic resources to the tender mercies of the Third World dictators who have so sorely mismanaged their own domestic economies. In this scheme the riches of the seabed would be administered by an international agency composed of the governments of the world — in which the "developing" countries would be of course over-represented. Moreover, the philosophy under which this administration would take place is collectivism, "equity," and denigration of marketplace incentives. The firms in a position to develop the resources of the oceans, mainly from western-oriented industrialized nations, would not be able to directly profit from their efforts. On the contrary, the fruits of their labor would have to be shared by all, since the oceans would not be considered private property, but rather the "common heritage of all mankind."[38]

The infant formula controversy arose when Nestles began marketing a breast milk substitute in the Third World. This led to the deaths of numerous infants, *not* because of any imperfection of the product; instead, this was due to the failures of Third World governments to live up to their self-appointed tasks of providing pure water, education (so that the consumers could read Nestles' directions), fuel (to warm up the milk) and electricity and other social overhead capital (for refrigeration of the milk when not in use). As a result of this fiasco the U.N., with an overwhelming vote from the governments responsible for the tragedy in the first place, successfully shifted blame, at least in the eyes of opinion molders, from themselves to this unfortunate multinational corporation.[39]

And as far as the U.N. developing a conduct code for the MNCs, this agency would do better to get its own house in order, and remember the aphorism about people who live in glass houses (literally, in this case) casting stones.

Paul Heyne analyzes the MNC phenonenon as follows:

> The premise that runs throughout the section on the United States and the world economy (#s 270-319) is that 'transnational corporations' pursue profits and are therefore likely to do harm when they enter Third World countries unless they are restrained by international agencies and national governments, which pursue the common good. (See especially #s 281,299,311). This is sheer prejudice. Greed, corruption, poor stewardship, and economic irresponsibility are generally under much more effective control in multinational corporations, as a result of ordinary competitive pressures, than they are in many national governments and even some United Nations agencies.[40]

Notes

1. Actually, the critique in BP of national boundaries is less straightforward and radical than might have been expected from a document which is presumably grounded in moral philosophy, and seeks to challenge political realities — let the chips fall where they may. The internationalism of the BP is qualified by the concession that national boundaries and interests can claim some legitimacy. As well, they state that ''economic policy cannot be governed by national goals alone'' (#269) when it would have been far better for an internationalist critique of the status quo to challenge the idea that national goals should have any relevance whatsoever.

2. Consider these statistics on national per capita income furnished by the bishops: ''Half of the world's population — 2.26 billion people — live in countries where the per capita annual income is the equivalent of $400 or less (U.S. per capita income is $12,530). Four hundred fifty million people are malnourished or facing

starvation, despite abundant harvests worldwide. Fifteen out of every 100 children born in these countries will die before the age of 5, and hundreds of thousands of the survivors will be stunted physically or mentally. The average life expectancy of these people (except for China) is 48 years (in the United States it is 74 years)'' (#274).

3. Another ''scandal'' unearthed by the bishops is that there are ''half a billion malnourished people in a world of aggregate surplus of food production'' (#313). This would seem to imply that we in the ''overdeveloped West'' (see Bob Goudzwaard, *Aid for the Overdeveloped West*, Toronto: Wedge Pub., 1975), were only able to grow this excess of foodstuffs by making it impossible for farmers in the underdeveloped Third World to harvest their own. It is as if there is only so much agricultural activity that can take place in the world at any given time, and that if ''we'' do more of it, less will be left for ''them.'' Nothing, of course, could be further from the truth. This modern day ''lump of agriculture'' argument is entirely without foundation. The reason food cannot readily be grown in the Third World is not because of magnificent productivity in the west, but because of the underdeveloped countries centralized planning, land ''reform,'' organized state land theft from profitable farmers (''kulaks,'' successful peasants, etc.) and price controls for agriculture produce which are sometimes so strict that resources (tractors, mules, feed, etc.) cost more than can be charged for the final farm goods. See in this regard Peter Bauer, *op. cit.*

4. Walter Block, ''Liberation Theology and the Economy,'' *Grail: An Ecumenical Journal*, Vol. 1, No. 3, September 1985, pp. 78-80.

5. *Ibid.*

6. Elsewhere, the bishops state: ''In view of the disadvantageous terms of trade under which the developing countries operate, we consider international trade as the testing ground of social justice for the developing countries'' BP, p. 341.

7. Mercantilism is the doctrine according to which a nation's wealth consists primarily of piling up huge excesses of exports over imports, so that gold (i.e., wealth) can accrue in the home country. It is indeed puzzling to find the bishops in support of a view which equates wealth with the scrooge-like hoarding of specie. To mix our metaphors, the mercantilists and their supporters might well benefit from perusing the tale of King Midas, or Adam Smith's *The Wealth of Nations*, which was written, in large part, as an antidote to mercantilism.

8. Walter Block, *Grail, op.cit.* p. 83.

9. As unfortunate as is this call for ''fair'' trade on the part of the bishops, it is ever so much more disappointing that the Lay Letter, too, uses the fairness ploy to buttress its I'm-for-free-trade-but ... stance. It is one thing when a relatively economically innocent group of church leaders fails to fully embrace a position of unfettered free enterprise in international relations; it is quite another when a sophisticated group of writers, who marshall the arguments for free trade eloquently and completely, makes this same mistake (see 25, p. 71).

There is another comparison between BP and Lay Letter which is more to the credit of the former than the latter. Consider the following statement: "Internationally, the bishops readily accept the image of 'Third World' nations as helpless victims of the more prosperous countries and call for expanded aid programs, easier loans, and revised trade patterns to redistribute wealth from north to south. The lay committee points to the striking differences between one 'third world' nation and another and argue that the key to overcoming poverty lies primarily within each nation, specifically in the attitudes and habits of its people and its government" (16, p.9). The Lay Letter is obviously correct in pointing to the attitudes of the people, and the policy of government, as prime determinations of economic development. But the point is, at least with regard to international trade, the poor nations *are* helpless victims of the restrictionist policies pursued by the Western industrialized countries. The Third World has no vote in a U.S. Congress or Canadian Parliament which places numerous tariff and non-tariff barriers against their exports to North America. And yet the underdeveloped nations suffer grievously from such a policy. Likewise, it is impossible to overstate the degree to which Third World government mismanagement is responsible for the economic disarray they rule over. And yet international trade restrictions is one area (perhaps the only one) where prime blame must rest at the door of the rich countries, not the poor. Had the BP made this point more clearly, it could have promoted the preferential option for the poor in an important way.

10. This, of course, is in sharp distinction to *free* trade, the doctrine that government shall not interfere in any way with international commerce.

11. It may be that a given trader is in dire circumstances, and is thus "forced" to engage in a certain commercial relationship (i.e., the starving man agrees to work for an exceedingly low salary). Even in this case, however, the trade is still of benefit to him. It is the circumstances, not the employer, which force him to "submit" to the deal. And if it did not improve his position, in his own eyes at least, he would not agree to participate.

12. The bishops also object to free trade on the ground that there are "great disparities in trading benefits that exist between the dominant industrialized countries and the developing countries" (#298). But this is unproven. Indeed, it cannot be proven. For the gains of trade are necessarily subjective. They are the trader's assessment of the difference in the employment or utility or value he placed on the goods to be gained and given up. All we can ever say is that each party to a trade benefits from it. We cannot compare the benefits. Thus, it is impossible in principle to provide scientific evidence for any such claim regarding "disparities in trading benefits." On this point, see Murray Rothbard, *Toward a Reconstruction of Utility and Welfare Economics*, New York: Center for Libertarian Studies, occasional paper #3, 1977.

13. There is only one further complication that needs to be considered here. Suppose Ruritania subsidizes its exports for the express purpose of undermining

the American widget industry. Then, when American widget makers have all gone bankrupt, the heinous Ruritanians can double or triple their prices, thus exploiting the American consumer. Are not countervailing tariffs justified in this case? No. First of all this argument reckons without the possibility that other countries may also produce widgets; when the Ruritanians cut back on production in order to raise their prices, the Americans can make their purchases elsewhere. In addition, American entrepreneurs who suspect the Ruritanians of such "villainy" may subsidize their own widget production, even against the "unfair" imports. True, they will lose money in the short run, while the Ruritanian government is subsidizing low prices but they can treat these expenditures as an investment. For when the "evil" Ruritanians show their true colors, these businessmen can burst forth, and make great profits. Even better, all these far-sighted men of commerce need do is maintain their widget factories on a stand-by basis; at very little cost, they can thus stand ready to re-enter the industry, thwarting the ultimate Ruritanian plan, at great profits to themselves. See in this regard, John McGee, "Predatory Price Cutting: The Standard Oil Case,": *Journal of Law and Economics*, Vol. 1, October 1958, pp. 137-169.

14. One commentator who is very sharply critical of other sections of the BP agrees at least with its view that there is conflict between free trade and domestic employment. Says Peter L. Berger, "The U.S. should devise more favorable trade arrangements with Third World countries: definitely, but any such trade benefits to the Third World would be in tension ... with the goal of full employment for Americans that the bishops endorse ..." (see 3, p. 34). See also Andrew Greely, who states, "The hierarchy et al. want the United States, at the same time it lowers trade barriers, to diminish the level of structural or frictional unemployment. They show no signs of comprehending that if you lower barriers, let us say, to Trinidadian steel and Brazilian automobiles, you will put workers in Port of Spain and Sao Paulo in direct competition with workers in south Chicago and Detroit. In any such competition the inefficient American industries will suffer, and structural unemployment will increase. How do you balance these two highly desirable economic goals?" (see 14, p. 36).

15. Why, then, it will be readily asked, does mankind suffer from chronic unemployment? The causes are legion, but virtually all of them may be laid at the door of unwise government policy. Even a partial listing must include the following:
   1. Policies which artificially boost wage rates beyond productivity levels and thus price people out of the labor market:
      a. minimum wage law
      b. unions
      c. "fair" wage enactments
      d. equal pay for equal work legislation
      e. equal pay for work of equal value
      f. working conditions requirements
      g. employee "protection" (no firing without "due process")

2. Policies which subsidize unemployment and/or compete with employment:
    a. unemployment insurance
    b. government training programs (which pay people to prepare for jobs which may well not exist when they graduate)
    c. welfare payments
3. Taxes on employment:
    a. payroll taxes
    b. employment taxes
    c. income taxes
    d. tariffs (a tax on jobs in the export sector)
4. Regulations which prohibit employment:
    a. taxi medallions
    b. anti-peddling laws
    c. zoning codes which prohibit commerce
5. Laws which reduce labor mobility:
    a. rent control
    b. intra and international trade barriers (buy local policies)
    c. immigration restrictions
6. Fiscal policy:
    a. inflation
    b. monetary shocks
    c. sharp government expenditure changes
7. Changing conditions:
    a. changes in supply
    b. changes in demand
    c. changes in taste
    d. economic development
    e. sharp population growth
    f. sharp changes in labor force participation
(Note that in categories 1-6 it is government that creates unemployment; only in section 7 may be found sources of (temporary) joblessness intrinsic to a free marketplace.)

16. Strictly speaking, foreigners would not be giving gifts; rather, they would be accepting oblong green colored pieces of paper with lots of zeroes on them in trade for their exports. Weird people, these foreigners.

17. Suppose the foreigners come bearing gifts with the express intention of undermining U.S. industry and then "profiteering" when the Americans have been brought to a position of servile dependence on further largesse. We have already dealt with this objection above. See Chapter VI, footnote 12.

18. Statistics for 1980 are found in *Statistical Abstract of the United States, 1984*, 10th Ed., U.S. Department of Commerce, Bureau of the Census, table no. 669, p. 405; for 1880, in *Historical Statistics of the United States: Colonial Times to 1970*, Part 1, U.S. Department of Commerce, Bureau of the Census, table D11-25, p. 127.

19. See Gary Becker, *Human Capital*, New York: National Bureau of Economic Research, 1984.

20. We have already established that jobs for all these people shall be found in the industries which supply the needs of the Japanese or Southeast Asian. Here, we are only concerned to analyze the incidence of the dislocation caused by these changes.

21. This is the non-pejorative phraseology suggested by Peter Bauer as a substitute for "foreign aid."

22. While on the subject of prejudicial terminology, we cannot forebear to mention several other instances. We do so in the following format: first column, the term in current oxymoronic use; second, a non-pejorative rendition; third, a translation into what might be considered more accurate language.

oxymoron	neutral, non-pejorative	accurate translation
developing countries	non-developing countries	retrogressing countries
public education	a system whereby governments compel citizens to pay taxes for services labelled "educational," and then make these services available for "free"	public miseducation
protectionism	government interferences or obstacles with international trade	destructionism
freeways	government financed and managed highways	taxways
airline food	food-like substances served on airplanes	swill
equity	equality	a scheme to forcibly transfer income from rich to poor, which reduces the incentive of both to earn income
military intelligence	military statistics	military confusion

Were we to present "foreign aid" in this format, it would read: foreign aid/government-to-government transfers of funds/payments to dictators of economically retrogressing countries to enable them to purchase monuments, machine guns and Mercedes — and to allow their enactment of Marxist-oriented central planning policies while staving off the starvation that inevitably follows in the wake of all such schemes for a few short years.

One might think that advocates of government-to-government transfers of income, such as the bishops, might welcome our lexicographical innovations, particularly with regard to developing/non-developed/retrogressing countries. For the first appellation implies that the nation in question is doing quite well thank you, and therefore it is not really in need of "aid." In contrast, the second of the two, and especially the third, give the very clear impression that "help" is urgently required.

23. States Paul Heyne: "They urge increased foreign aid, for example, which they say, 'gets an increasingly bad press in the United States' (#307). They nowhere point out that foreign aid has also been severely criticized, from the left as well as the right, for the harm that it often does to the cause of economic development, especially development in directions that might raise the living standards of the poorest people in so-called Third World countries. Aid from governments goes largely to governments. The Letter generally assumes, contrary to an abundance of readily available evidence, that government officials in poor countries will use foreign aid in just and constructive ways" (see 15, p.10).

24. Says Andrew M. Greely on this topic: "The bishops unhesitatingly call for a greater transfer of funds to Third World countries, a position that, on the face of it, seemed obviously Christian. Yet some students of the problem including some economists in the less developed countries, think that most such transfers are not healthy and do more harm than good to the receiving nations" (see 14, p. 36).

25. Our analysis relies heavily on the following literature: *The Economics of Underdeveloped Countries*, by P.T. Bauer and B.S. Yamey, Chicago: University of Chicago Press, 1957; *Equality, the Third World and Economic Delusion* by P.T. Bauer, Cambridge: Harvard University Press, 1984; "Western Guilt and Third World Poverty," by P.T. Bauer (*Commentary*, January 1976); "Against the New Economic Order" by P.T. Bauer and B.S. Yamey (*Commentary*, April 1977); "Foreign Aid for What?" by P.T. Bauer and John O'Sullivan (*Commentary*, December 1978); "East-West/North-South" by P.T. Bauer and B.S. Yamey (*Commentary*, September 1980); *Development Without Aid: Growth, Prosperity and Government*, by Melvyn B. Krauss, N.Y.: McGraw Hill, 1983; *Reality and Rhetoric: Studies in the Economics of Development*, by P.T. Bauer, Cambridge: Harvard University Press, 1984; "Liberation Theology and Third World Development," by P.T. Bauer, in *Theology, Third World Development and Economic Justice*, Walter Block and Donald Shaw, eds., Vancouver: The Fraser Institute, 1985, pp. 35-38, 49-66.

26. Bauer and Yamey, *ibid.*, (*Commentary*, p. 38, September 1985).

27. *Ibid.*, p. 39.

28. *Ibid.*, p. 39.

29. *Op. cit.*, footnote 24. The bishops claim that "economic infrastructure — roads, transportation, communication, education, health, etc. ... are not profit-making enterprises and therefore do not attract much private capital, but without them no real economic growth can take place" (#310). Krause has shown one difficulty with this view. In addition, we must consider the point that while investment infrastructure — like all other successful investments—can indeed be productive, when the presently developed countries were first undergoing economic growth, many of these capital goods were financed by *private* enterprise, not by government.

30. See Donald Armstrong, *Monopoly vs. Competition*, Vancouver: The Fraser Institute, 1982.

31. "Equitable distribution" of benefits, of course, holds no interest to the typical "developing" country's government.

32. In the view of equity maintained by the philosophy of negative rights (see section II above), an equitable investment is one which does not commit violence against non-initiators of force. Thus, all MNC activity *except* that which "help(s) ... maintain an oppressive elite in power" is certainly "equitable." What about those international firms which do help maintain oppressive elites in power? Strictly speaking, these must be deemed inequitable. But any such ruling must apply not only to most countries in Africa, and many in South America and Asia, but also to investments behind the Iron and Bamboo Curtains. Do the bishops suggest cutting off all trade with the Soviet Union and its satellites?

33. States Donald Warwick: "On the question of developing countries, the Lay Letter is in some respects much more specific than the bishops. And the specific recommendation is that the developing countries should adopt in all cases free economies or capitalist economies and avoid statist solutions to economic problems. The letter argues that most of the problems of developing countries are caused not by lack of resources, not by excess population or similar phenomena, but by governmental mismanagement. And the mismanagement is presumably the highest in those countries that have the greatest involvement by the state. The letter argues that rich nations do not cause the poverty of the poor nations. The poor nations bring it on themselves by failure to use the resources that they have, including human resources" (see 19, p. 110).

34. Of course, no MNC can take any business decisions without permission of the group that happens to have seized power in the underdeveloped country. So in a sense, the bishops' call for joint control could be interpreted as a demand for something that would take place in any case. But in a profound sense, to the extent of the moral authority of the BP (and it is formidable), this demand may further stiffen the backbones of host country governments, and strengthen

their demands for a say in MNC investments. Should this eventuality actually occur, the bishops would be (indirectly) responsible for yet another decrease in the welfare of the struggling poor in the Third World.

35. Indeed, the BP itself vociferously objects to such a policy (see #275 and text discussion supra).

36. True, there was the nationalization of the Suez Canal of Egypt. But did any British politicians lose their own money in this takeover? Hardly. The money spent on this project was not their own in the first place, but rather that of the mulcted U.K. taxpayers.

37. It is no accident that even the rich people from the Third World ofttimes decline to invest locally, preferring Swiss bank accounts or apartment blocks in North America. To coin a phrase, they fear to tread where the angelic MNCs dare to rush in (see 25, p. 66).

38. For further reading on this topic, see Doug Bandow, "Developing the Mineral Resources of the Seabed," *Cato Journal*, Vol. 2, No. 3, Winter 1982, pp. 793-821; Roger Brooks, "The Law of the Sea Treaty: Can the U.S. Afford to Sign?" Backgrounder, The Heritage Foundation, June 7, 1982, p. 19, CRS, pp. 66-67; William Pendley, "The U.S. Will Need Seabed Minerals," Oceanus 25 (Fall 1982); Terry L. Anderson, "The New Resource Economics: Old Ideas and New Applications," *American Journal of Agricultural Economics*, 64, no. 5, 1983; Jack Hirshleifer, James C. DeHaven and Jerome W. Milliman, *Water Supply Economics Technology Policy*, Chicago: The University of Chicago Press, 1960; Terry L. Anderson, ed., *Water Resources: Bureaucracy, Property Rights, and the Environment*, Cambridge, Mass.: Pacific Institute for Public Policy Research and Ballinger Publishing Co., 1983; James Johnston, "Petroleum Revenue Sharing from Seabeds Beyond 200 Miles Offshore," *Marine Technology Society Journal 14*, 1980, pp. 28-30; David Johnson and Dennis Logue, "Economic Interests in Law of the Sea Issues," in Amacher and Sweeney, eds., *The Law of the Sea U.S. Interests and Alternatives*, Washington, D.C.: American Enterprise Institute, 1976; Fred Singer, "The Great UN Snorkel," *The American Spectator*, May 1981, p. 24; William Hawkins, "Reaffirming Freedom of the Seas," *The Freeman*, March 1982; James Johnston, "The Economics of the Common Heritage of Mankind," *Marine Technology Journal 13*, December 1979-January 1980; GAO, pp. 32-33: Singer, Alan Abelson, "Who Buried the Law of the Sea?," *Barron's*, July 26, 1982, p. 19.

39. See in this regard Walter Block, "Comment on Theological Perspectives on Economics," *Morality of the Marketplace: Religious and Economic Perspectives*, Vancouver: The Fraser Institute, 1985, pp. 83-87.

40. See 15, p. 10. "Some" United Nations agencies?

CHAPTER 7

CONCLUSION

We shall conclude this commentary with a brief venture into the realm of theology, which is sure to be fraught with all sorts of dangers, both spiritual and temporal.

The last sentence of BP reads as follows: "In (this) love and friendship, God is glorified and God's grandeur revealed"(#333). Consider for a moment only the final three words, "God's grandeur revealed." Where else is "God's grandeur revealed?"

Clerics, ecclesiastics, religious people, have seen the work of the Lord in numerous realms. In mathematics, in biology, in physics, in painting, in sculpture, in sunsets, in the perfection of diamonds. In all of these areas, people have seen great beauty, much complexity — and coupled with a simplicity so serene that it appears as if the hand of a Higher Power is at work. In a similar vein, in the movie *Amadeus*, Salieri said "If God spoke to man, it would be through the music of Mozart." And in the movie *Chariots of Fire*, one of the protagonists said that the grandeur of God is revealed in foot races.

God, in short, is everywhere, in this view.[1] And this leads to a final criticism of BP. There is no appreciation, in this document, that the hand of a Greater Being is also at work in the free market. There is no recognition that the "invisible hand," too, is part of God's plan. There is no awe, not even any recognition of the magical, spiritual dimension, of the pure pristine beauty, of the marketplace.[2]

This, perhaps, is the greatest flaw of BP.

Notes

1. I owe this point to Mr. Jim Johnston, of Standard Oil and Economic Education for the Clergy, Inc., Bethesda, Maryland.

2. I trust it will be seen as no more idolatrous to perceive the hand of God in the free enterprise system, than to see it in mathematics, music, athletics, etc.

APPENDIX

The overwhelming majority of the points made in this assessment of the First Draft of the U.S. Bishops' Pastoral "Catholic Social Teaching and the U.S. Economy,"[1] have been critical; indeed, highly critical. It therefore behooves us to balance matters by mentioning as well the positive elements of the Bishops' Pastoral. In addition, we offer several defenses in response to the sometimes unjust criticism levelled against BP by other commentators.

I. MORAL COURAGE

High on any list of the praiseworthy aspects of BP is the moral courage it took to contemplate this project, do the research, and publish it. Moral courage, moreover, pervades every nook and cranny of this document. The bishops have a point of view, which they hold strongly, and they do not hesitate to deliver their message in a forthright and even forceful manner.[2]

The bishops had anticipated that their pastoral letter would unleash a torrent of harsh criticism,[3] and in the event this expectation was not disappointed. But even they may not have realized the level of vilification their epistle would call forth. A survey of the reaction reveals the following commentaries: "palpable nonsense,"[4] "moralistic drivel,"[5] and "meddling."[6] "Hypocrisy" was the most popular charge, mentioned on literally dozens of occasions in the literature that is beginning to spring up in reaction to BP. The Catholic Church, it appears from this criticism, has not put its own house fully in order, and should hold its tongue until such time as it has done so — and done so perfectly.[7] For example, BP advocates massive income transfers from rich to poor, and yet it itself remains a wealthy institution.[8] The bishops are also castigated for hypocrisy on the grounds that they have not promoted unions, equal pay, and affirmative action for employees of the Catholic Church.[9]

There are several ways to refute these charges. First of all, the bishops themselves admit that the Church, too, is an economic actor, albeit an imperfect one, and that as such, it too should struggle[10] to incorporate the teachings of BP into its own behaviour (#s143-150). This includes the recognition of the rights of Church employees to organize for purposes of collective bargaining. State the bishops, "the church would be justly accused of hypocrisy and scandal were any of its agencies to try to prevent the organization of unions ..." (#148).[11] And according to Bishop Weakland, the chairman of the committee which prepared BP, "the letter 'will not be credible' without an examination of the church's role in the economy including its relationships with employees ...."[12]

It is true that people will tend to disbelieve BP unless the Church begins to act in conformity with its teachings. However, there is a far more basic refutation of the charge of hypocrisy available to the bishops. This consists of showing that all such complaints are merely variants of the *ad hominem* argument, an informal fallacy in logic.

Let us assume just for the sake of argument that the bishops were indeed hypocritical, saying one thing and doing another. Even so, this is all beside the point. Our task, here, is to evaluate the truth of BP, and the economic activities of the bishops are entirely irrelevant to the veracity of their letter. Consider an analogy from the realm of morality. If a clergyman preaches against adultery, but is himself an adulterer, he may well lose the moral authority to pronounce on the subject, but the truth value of his statement holds regardless of his own actions. In like manner, the correctness of BP (or lack of same), is completely independent of the economic actions of its authors, and it is the former, not the latter, which is the subject of our present deliberations.

II. FREE SPEECH

Expertise

Secondly, the bishops are to be congratulated upon their refusal to bow down to demands that they impose restrictions on their rights of free speech. What were the reasons put forward in order to silence the bishops? One common criticism is that the bishops lack economic expertise.[13] So compelling is this argument that even so able a defender of BP as Brown accepts it, when he concedes that apart from the fact that the bishops have held hearings with experts in all parts of the country, it could reasonably be suggested that they were "venturing beyond their depth."[14]

But this is the veriest of nonsense. First of all, the argument from lack of expertise, like its colleague, the charge of hypocrisy, is an *argumentum ad hominem*, and therefore fallacious. The bishops may lack expertise, they may even be functionally illiterate, and yet the BP may still be correct in all its claims. The credentials of the authors are entirely irrelevant to the truth of their product, and this alone is our concern.

As well, it is by no means clear that the bishops lack expertise in economics. True, not a one of them has earned a Ph.D. in economics, but since when has this become the criterion of expertise? There are numerous economists of renown — such as Adam Smith, John Locke, and John Stuart Mill in years gone by and Gordon Tullock, Kenneth Boulding and David Friedman in the modern era — who cannot boast of an advanced degree in this discipline. Should we go to the ludicrous extreme of setting up a licensing authority, which would prohibit all but duly "qualified" persons from advancing their opinions on matters economic?[15]

Then, too, there is the fact that BP very closely resembles the work of well-known and presumably "expert" economists such as Robert Heilbroner, Robert Lekachman, and John Kenneth Galbraith. If these writers are economic experts, and BP is comparable to their publications, on this criterion we must grant that the bishops have as much expertise as these other laborers in the vineyards of economics.

In one variant of this charge of lack of expertise, Dwyer states "When the bishops engage in special pleading for particular solutions, they are not speaking as bishops. They are espousing a particular political position and in so doing they exceed their competence."[16] But this opens up the embarrassing question of just who could make a statement such as BP without exceeding their competence? It could not be economists, for this discipline is a positive one, specializing in such "if ... then" questions as "What are the causes of inflation, poverty, etc.?," "If price changes, and all other factors remain constant, what will result?"[17] This being the case, the much decried and so-called lack of economic expertise on the part of the bishops might actually be an asset, not a drawback. And if the requisite expertise is that of a philosopher or an ethicist, then the bishops' claim to this sort of knowledge is as good as that of anyone else, and superior to many.

Dwyer, moreover, is a theologian. How then can he be competent (on the spurious grounds of expertise favoured by some of the critics of BP) to know whether or not the bishops are well-versed in economics, philosophy, ethics or anything else for that matter, apart from theology?

In yet another variation on this theme, Paul Heyne claims that "those who claim to be speaking in behalf of the poor and the oppressed have an obligation to be competent social analysts ...."[18]

With regard to this dubious claim, we might ask if those who claim to be speaking for the rich have a similar and equal obligation to be ''competent analysts?'' If not, why not? There is also the question of why economists do not address their colleagues in such an *ad hominem* manner even when most vociferously disagreeing with each other. That is, one economist when criticizing the work of another, at least in print, is almost certain to stick to the issues at hand, and not venture into the perilous waters of antecedents, competence, and expertise. Could Heyne's objection be most sensibly interpreted as an attempt to circle the wagons and close ranks against outsiders?

And why is it incumbent on the bishops only to be competent economists? They speak out on numerous other not strictly theological issues as well: the family, birth control, mores, war. Since the bishops are not professional sociologists, biologists, experts in international relations, the Dwyer and Heyne objections would effectively muzzle the bishops in all areas, if followed. [19]

Trespass

Next, we consider the view that the bishops should hold their tongues because they do not have a ''mandate'' to speak out on economic issues. This charge is made by Peter L. Berger as follows: ''A common assumption of democracy is that no one has a 'mandate' (prophetic or otherwise) to speak for people who have not elected him as their spokesman; the Catholic bishops of the United States have not been elected by any constituency of poor people.'' [20] Lawler speaks of ''trespass'' in this regard: ''the Catholic tradition involves a clear division of labor: bishops are to proclaim general moral principles; the political chore of enacting those principles falls to Catholic laymen. So when the bishops endorse specific public policies, they are trespassing on the layman's territory.'' [21]

The bishops have anticipated this objection, however. In their conclusion, especially #s 321-3, 325 and 330, they warn against a ''spiritually schizophrenic existence'' (#330) in which, in effect, people apply their moral and religious precepts on the Sabbath — but not during the working days of the week. Were the bishops to ''stick to their knitting,'' e.g., confine themselves to discussing proper Sabbath behaviour, etc., they would only be exacerbating this unfortunate bifurcation. If this is what the division of labor requires, then so much the worse for the division of labor. [22]

Harm

The litany of irrelevant criticism has by no means been exhausted. There is also the claim that BP will do irreparable harm to numerous other goals, and therefore should never have been written. Negative consequences of this document, it is charged, include the "squandering of moral authority,"[23] "encouraging class conflict," or "divisiveness."[24] With regard to the bishops' moral authority, critics must realize that if the higher Church authorities had so little confidence in the men who presently occupy the U.S. bishopric offices, as implied by this "friendly" criticism, they presumably would be replaced.[25]

But let us suppose for the moment that the critic's fears are well placed (as was argued above) and that BP will compromise the moral authority of the U.S. bishops. Would it really have been better if the Pastoral Letter had not been written? Given that BP is an accurate portrayal of the bishops' thoughts,[26] is it not far better that their convictions on these matters see the light of day, there to be criticized in honest and open dialogue, rather than be suppressed out of fear? In other words, if the moral authority of the bishops is so reduced by BP, is it not better, more open and honest (even from the point of view of their loyal opposition) that they lose this benefit, to which they are not entitled in any case? With regard to the "harm" of divisiveness, Robert McAfee Brown offers two worthwhile responses. First, he points out, "church unity can be bought at too high a price." Secondly, he states, "truth emerges in the course of creative exchange."[27]

Catholic economics

Another presumed reason for the bishops to maintain a dignified silence on economic issues is the development record of "Catholic" nations. States Charles Krauthammer,

> Catholicism's historical record as a frame for economic development is not particularly encouraging. One has only to compare Protestant North America to Catholic South and Central America, or Quebec (before it declericalized itself in the 1960s) to the rest of Canada, to make the point gently. No one has yet accused the Catholic ethic of being a source of economic dynamism.[28]

Brown's reply to this effrontery is so good it deserves repetition (almost) in full:

> If the premise is correct that the Catholic Church has a bad track record in this regard, that is all the more reason to tackle the subject matter and begin to set things straight, so that errors will not be perpetuated. The bishops surely owe the faithful at least that ... .[29]

Motive mongering

The last group of attacks on BP we shall discuss attempts to account for the waywardness of this document in terms of special — and rather peculiar — motivations ascribed to its authors. The great emphasis in BP on the state, in preference to the marketplace, is alleged to spring from the fact that the Catholic Church is itself organized along hierarchical lines, and is therefore conducive to and reminiscent of the public sector.[30] Another rationale for the pro-government slant of BP is the supposition that if its policy prescriptions are followed, that is, if the U.S. moves from capitalism to socialism, there will be a greater role for the bishops to play in society.[31] Even geography has been suggested as the root of BP's leftist tinge: because of the location of the Conference of Bishops in Washington, D.C.[32] The most cryptic explanation of BP's policy orientation relates to the monastic background of Archbishop Weakland.[33]

The problem with motive mongering in all these forms and variations is the difficulty in knowing whether the correct explanation has been reached. How, after all, would one determine whether or not BP can best be understood as monasticism, or hierarchy writ large? Moreover, motive mongering is irrelevant to the truth or falsity of BP, which must be the primary concern in analyzing this document.

This section can best be summed up by contrasting two polar opposite views on the propriety of the bishops speaking out on economics. According to Archbishop Weakland, "the church's position (is) that no area of life is exempt from moral evaluation and judgment."[34] In contrast, states von Geusau, a theologian from the Netherlands, "Only in exceptional circumstances — such as the bishops of Poland encounter — should bishops address themselves to governments with policy recommendations."[35] Between these two statements, little accommodation is possible. One pictures the Catholic Church as an ostrich, with its head in the sand, the other as an eagle, soaring on high, unafraid to look at all beneath it. It is difficult to understand how such different visions could be urged upon the Catholic Church by two of its sons.

III. MORAL INDIGNATION

The third positive element of BP is its sense of outrage. The bishops are not cold and dispassionate in their assessment of the U.S. economy. There are injustices in the business world,[36] there are victims in the economic sphere,[37] and when these phenomena arise in the course of discussion, it is almost incumbent upon any analysis with a strong moral dimension to express at least a measure of indignation.

For example, according to James Hitchcock,

> The bishops' letter does convey a certain sense of moral urgency, insisting that dire poverty and injustice are unacceptable to Christians, and its greatest strength is its unflinching insistence that every kind of public policy must be rigorously scrutinized with regard to its effects on the poor.[38]

IV. PREFERENTIAL OPTION FOR THE POOR

The bishops are to be congratulated for making the welfare of the poor a bedrock of their moral and economic analysis. In so doing, they redirect public consciousness toward an examination of the causes and cures of poverty, and this can, if followed through carefully, only be to the good. In future studies of society, thanks to BP, it shall be exceedingly difficult to avoid the perspective of the last, least and lost amongst us; commentators shall be led, by the very visible hand of the bishops, to ask of each proposed policy, what are its implications for the poor?[39]

However, care must be exercised not to misinterpret this doctrine. We must not conclude justice can be fully satisfied by a fair treatment of the poor. Surely there is more to justice than proper treatment for the poverty stricken.

The preferential option for the poor, properly interpreted, may be a necessary condition for justice, but it is hardly a sufficient one.[40] In this regard, the statement of this option in the Lay Letter is far superior to that which obtains in BP. According to the former, "*One* measure of a good society is how well it cares for the weakest and most vulnerable of its members"[41] (emphasis added).

In view of the latter, "The justice of a community is measured by its treatment of the poor and the powerless in society."[42]

Another caveat. We cannot interpret the preferential option for the poor as carte blanche for those with low incomes, vis-a-vis the wealthy. For example, only the opposite of justice is served if a person who inhabits territory south of the poverty line robs at gunpoint a rich but honest man.[43]

Consider two other mis-statements of this option: "The needs of the poor take priority over the desires of the rich" (#106, quoting Pope John Paul II) and "government economic policies must ensure that the poor have their basic needs met before less basic desires of others are satisfied."[44] Paul Heyne has quite properly criticized these misinterpretations as follows:

"This is perilously close to pure demagoguery. Is the government supposed to call a halt to all skiing (surely a luxury) until everyone in the society
is receiving a sound education (deemed a necessity by the bishops)? If it
doesn't mean something like this, what does it mean ...?"[45]

V. EXPLOITATION

One of the most praiseworthy aspects of BP is its keen awareness that the
U.S. economy contains numerous instances of exploitation. Even more important, the bishops are cognizant of the fact that where there is economic
injustice, there must be perpetrators of such injustice. Profound as is this
insight, the authors of BP are to be congratulated upon it even the more,
given that two of their prominent neo-conservative detractors not only missed
it, but took great pains to distance themselves from it.[46]

    First, let us document the bishops' appreciation of the phenomenon of
exploitation, injustice, and responsibility:

> We must also reflect more concretely on who is actually responsible
> for bringing about the necessary changes. Our society is highly com-
> plex and so is the apportionment of rights and responsibilities for shap-
> ing economic life. Nor do these responsibilities and rights pertain solely
> to individual persons. Persons act within institutions, such as
> agricultural enterprises, small businesses, corporations, labor unions,
> service agencies, banks and the government. These institutions pro-
> vide individuals with distinct sorts of power to promote or impede the
> achievement of justice. Therefore in determining who is responsible
> for what in economic life we must attend to these institutional con-
> texts and also ask whether certain changes in the prevailing institu-
> tional roles may be called for. To this end, we now want to indicate
> how various kinds of economic actors, both individual and institutional,
> can foster greater economic justice (#107,108).

The bishops herein serve notice that there are individuals, (specific people, not some vague "society") who are responsible for the evils perpetrated
on the poor.

    Next, consider the bishops' analysis of income transfers: "If one added
in such benefits to the non-poor as veterans allowances, loans for higher
education and support for farm prices, it would be clear that the middle
classes receive far more from the federal government than do the poor"
(#224).

    "If we are honest, those of us who have enough will have to admit that
we receive far more from the government than do those on welfare" (#240).

Corporate welfare bums

The bishops have touched only the tip of the iceberg. There are literally hundreds cf programs which subsidize, protect or "regulate" the rich and upper middle class to their benefit, and to the detriment of the more populous lower middle class and poor. "Corporate welfare bums" is a phrase that neatly summarizes the welter of bailouts, licensing arrangements, guarantees, restrictive entry provisions, tariff and other import protections, union legislation, and minimum wage laws which transfer vast sums of money from the threadbare pockets of the poor to the ermine-wrapped coffers of the rich and relatively well-to-do.

But Michael Novak, for one, is having none of this. In his view:

> The bishops speak of the 'causes of poverty,' as if wealth were the natural condition of human beings and as if to be poor is to be held back by external others, both individuals and institutions. It is as if poverty is a form of positive oppression by others. It is as if, for the bishops, the poor are being done to, being held back, and as if, chains being lifted, they would rise by natural tendency into wealth. Thus, the bishops speak of poverty in America as a 'social and moral scandal' as if it were the fault of American institutions and of those of the American people who are not poor.[47]

> (The bishops' use of the term) 'marginalization' suggests a deliberate policy — people being driven to the margins. Or at least an intention to keep people invisible or out of sight.[48]

> Correlatively, in speaking of the poor, the draft (BP) tends to look at the poor as passive victims ....[49]

> But the implied image (in BP) of the economy is that of a ... managed economy, whose 'priorities' are set by experts standing outside the system and directing it consciously from above.[50]

Contrary to the claim of Novak, however, these views of the bishops are correct. Anyone who seriously contends that the poor are not "held back" and "done to" has somehow failed to take into account the work of numerous economists who have shown, in detail, just how a deliberative and interventionistic government has "chained," despoiled, oppressed and violated the rights of millions of poor people in the U.S. In *The State Against Blacks*, for instance, Walter Williams demonstrates how minimum wage and union legislation, taxicab licensing systems, and street vendor laws — passed by legislators with due deliberation — deprive thousands of poor citizens of a livelihood.[51] But we need not seek elsewhere for studies which show the deleterious effects of government intervention into the economy on the poor. The numerous books of Michael Novak himself brilliantly show this over and over and over again.[52]

Negative Impact

Paul Heyne is another critic of BP who for some inexplicable reason turns his back on a brilliant career of demonstrating that government interference impacts negatively on the poor. Heyne, too, takes the bishops to task for claiming that the poor are suffering from the activities of other, more powerful people. Says Heyne:

> ... the actual unemployment rate is the outcome of a social system rather than anyone's direct goal, it cannot be reduced in the way that we reduce a thermostat setting or the height of the kitchen shelf.[10]
>
> No one intends unemployment ....
>
> Throughout the (BP), the poor, the unemployed and the 'marginalized' are presented as persons compelled by forces beyond their control.
>
> ... in an economic system, results are not intended. Or, to put it another way, the results that emerge are not the results that were intended by the people who produced them.[53]

As in the case of Novak, Heyne's other writings contradict the above cited critique of BP. For example, he himself has elsewhere demonstrated that unemployment can be reduced by direct action (by repealing the minimum wage law), in exactly the same deliberate way as a thermostat might be adjusted.[54]

Novak and Heyne make two claims against the bishops. First, the poor are not helpless, or victimized, or compelled by more powerful forces. This, we have seen, must be rejected, based on evidence supplied not only by much of the economics profession, but by their own distinguished contribution to it as well. Their second claim, however, is more difficult to refute. Here, they deny the charge of the bishops that the destruction visited on the poor by and through government, is "intended," "goal-directed," "deliberate," "consciously directed," constitutes "positive oppression," etc.

Common sense

This claim cannot be so easily rejected because, for one thing, neo-classical economics[55] deals mainly with results of human action, not with the internal mind-states of the perpetrators. The issue, rather, is a matter of common sense, and here the bishops would appear to have a reasonable argument. In any case, if economics must remain forever more silent on the question of motivation, how is it that Novak and Heyne are so sure that none of these depredations on the poor are "directed," or "deliberate?"

These two critics speak as if the U.S. economy were presently one of *laissez-faire* capitalism. For if and only if there were a full free market in operation, would their claims be true; then, no one could exploit another (whether purposefully or not) through the apparatus of the state. But it is inexplicable that scholars of the mettle of Novak and Heyne should not be more aware of the activities of the rent-seeking transfer society[56] which are everywhere around us. The U.S. is now a mixed welfare state, one from which the rich gain in innumerable and illegitimate ways; it is not the one advocated by Adam Smith.

VI. HOW NATURAL IS WEALTH?

Another incisive point made in BP concerns the question of how natural — or artificial — is wealth. The bishops take the view that in the absence of any barriers to the contrary, the natural lot of mankind is one of prosperity.[57]

Michael Novak castigates the bishops for this position. States he,

> ... the bishops speak ... as if wealth were the natural condition of human beings ...."
>
> The point of view of the lay letter, by contrast, is that poverty is a common initial condition in human history, and that to create wealth, new causes such as investment, creativity, and entrepreneurship must be put into operation.[58]

Our answer to this dispute will of course depend on precisely how we define the natural state of affairs. In order to put the Novak hypothesis in a reasonable light,[59] we define "nature" in terms of a full free enterprise system, that is, no prohibitions of any kind over "capitalist acts between consenting adults"[60] shall be implemented. Under such conditions, what is the likely prosperity level of a group of people lacking all semblance of business sense, economic creativity, investment funds, or entrepreneurship? And the obvious answer is, they are likely to do very well, thank you.

Thanks to the "magic of the marketplace,"[61] such people do very well, even in America, a land which only very very imperfectly approaches a free marketplace. These are the millions of lower and middle class

Americans whose standard of living is the envy of the rest of the world, who yet have no funds invested in business, little creativity in the economic sense, and no personal acquaintance whatever with the entrepreneurial spirit. To be sure, the qualities mentioned by Novak are also important. But only a minority need have them, and this requirement has been met in virtually every society known to man. No. The bottleneck is not entrepreneurship, which grows like a hardy weed, and is everywhere abundant. What stifles economic growth is rather excessive government interference into the marketplace; this perverts, distorts and grinds down man's natural inclination toward prosperity and wealth.

VII. DIALOGUE

The bishops call for dialogue on the economic and moral questions which face us today. This is most welcome. It is by airing these issues — under the unique perspective offered to us in BP — that progress can be made. Already the process seems to be bearing fruit in terms of promoting discussion.[62] An immense critical literature has sprung up in the short time since the first appearance of BP. And the consultative procedure which will take place before the final version is published will likely encourage even more reflection.

Donald Warwick, consultant to the Bishops' Committee expresses himself on this matter as follows:

> For in the end, what we want in this debate is an opportunity for intelligent people who may have different points of view on how this country should be organized to express their views, to be understood with respect by others who may disagree with those points of view, so that in the end the Catholic bishops and all the rest of us have an opportunity to issue some intelligent recommendations and to form some intelligent opinions about what the United States economy should look like.[63]

According to Brown,

> The draft is a model of clarity. Its style is both crisp and passionate, its structure is clear and its documentation is extensive, drawn not only from church teaching but from a wide spectrum of contemporary sources. Any notion that the letter is nothing but a collection of left-wing cliches is belied not only by the tone, but by the sources cited to sustain the descriptive material in the text.[64]

The BP does read well, but the widespread representation of its sources and consultants along the political economic spectrum leaves much to be desired. Conspicuous by their absence are the following eminent public policy analysts: Martin Anderson, Peter Bauer, Gary Becker, James Buchanan, William F. Buckley, Harold Demsetz, Milton Friedman, George Gilder, Henry Hazlitt, Melvyn Krauss, Irving Kristol, Charles Murray, Robert Nozick, Michael Novak, Murray Rothbard, George Stigler, Thomas Sowell, Gordon Tullock.

It is fervently to be hoped that greater representation from these advocates of freer markets will be sought in the next round in the ongoing process of dialogue.

VIII. IMMORALITY OF UNEMPLOYMENT

One can read numerous economic treatises without ever once coming across a claim to the effect that unemployment is immoral. Perhaps this is as it should be, given the division of labor which restricts the dismal science from normative concerns. Nevertheless, it is like a breath of fresh air to be told in blunt terms that "Current levels of unemployment are morally unjustified."[65]

Thanks to the U.S. bishops, we shall henceforth see not only the economic, sociological and psychological tragedies of unemployment, but we shall be able to view this phenomenon through a moral perspective as well.

There is a fly in the ointment, however. It is one thing to condemn present unemployment rates as immoral, and to describe a rate of 6-7 percent as "unacceptable" (#179), but it is quite another matter to reward a passing ethical grade to unemployment at the 3-4 percent level.[66] At what point does unemployment pass from "morally unjustified" to morally acceptable? This distinction of the bishops would thus appear to be rather arbitrary.

A more appropriate analytical device might be to distinguish between voluntary and involuntary unemployment. How can such a distinction be made?

An employment contract is nothing but a specific type of trade: one in which the employee gives up leisure and obtains money, and the employer pays the money and receives labor services in return. Involuntary or coercive employment, then, is the result of any barrier, such as the threat or actual use of force to prevent the consummation of an employment agreement. Examples include the minimum wage law, labour legislation which physically prevents the employer from hiring a strike breaker ("scab"), or union violence to that same end, as well as taxi, trucking, peddler and other such enactments which prohibit employment. Voluntary unemployment, on the other hand, consists of joblessness in the absence of such constraints. For example, a person may be engaging in job search (frictional unemployment), or holding out for a higher salary than presently offered, might be "in between" jobs, or involved in an extended vacation.

With this characterization in mind, we can more readily distinguish between that unemployment which is morally justified, and that which is not: any coercive unemployment, whatsoever, that is, above zero, is immoral, and any voluntary unemployment, no matter how high, even up to 100 percent of the labor force, is morally acceptable.

IX. OVERPOPULATION

The last point upon which we wish to congratulate the bishops pertains to their refusal to be stampeded by the over-populationists, the Malthusians of the day,[67] into a call for birth control, whether by abortion[68] or not, in order to promote economic development.

It has been shown time and time again that there is very little statistical correlation, or causal relation, between dense or high population and poverty. True, India is poor and highly populated, while Kuwait is rich and underpopulated. But there are numerous examples of just the opposite situation. For example, there are "teeming masses" jammed, sardine-like, into their luxurious dwellings in Manhattan, Paris, Rome, London, Tokyo and San Francisco. Alternatively, there are countries where nary a person can ever be seen, that nonetheless wallow in dire poverty.[69]

The bishops are to be saluted for their refusal to go along with widely accepted opinion on this matter.

Notes

1. See 36, henceforth BP.

2. Several of the bishop's critics have noted this forceful style of presentation and have objected to it, calling for a softer, more muted mode of expression. In particular, they have called upon the bishops to express their findings with more "humility" (see 18, p. 49). No one, of course, can be against "humility." Nevertheless, this is still an improper criticism, for it is hardly applied to people with whom one agrees. In any case, there is no lack of humility or modesty in the BP. For example, in inviting a response to their letter, they "recognize that our efforts are limited and but a beginning" (#331). For a shorter com-

mentary on the BP, written by the present author, see "Neglect of the Marketplace: The Questionable Economics of America's Bishops," *Notre Dame Journal of Law, Ethics, & Public Policy*, 1986, forthcoming.

3. See 8.

4. See 33.

5. See 2.

6. See 7, p. 247.

7. Robert McAfee Brown very properly states that the charge of hypocrisy can be successfully refuted by changes in the economic management of the church (so as to conform with BP) that are "simultaneous rather than sequential" (6, p. 928).

8. See 31; 14, pp. 44. In 4, Tom Bethell launches what can only be considered an extremely harsh — not to say scurrilous — attack on the Catholic bishops for holding a conference in the sumptuous Washington, D.C. Hilton. And the more sober, responsible and respectable *Religion and Society Report*, 30, p. 8, instead of rebuking Bethell for the impropriety and excessiveness of his remarks, actually supports him.

9. See 12; 13; 14, p. 44.

10. This admission is certainly further evidence of the modesty and humility which can be found in BP.

11. See 5, p. 130.

12. See 13.

13. See 19, p. 102; 14, p. 33; 30, p. 5; 12.

14. See 6, p. 927.

15. For a critique of licensing in the health field, see Ronald Hamowy, *Canadian Medicine: A Study in Restricted Entry*, Vancouver: The Fraser Institute, 1984.

16. See 10, p. 20.

17. Such positive economic analysis must be sharply distinguished from normative economics, which deals with such matters as "Is it justified to transfer wealth from rich to poor?," "What is the best trade off between production and distribution?" See in this regard Milton Friedman, *Essays on Positive Economics*, Chicago: University of Chicago Press, 1953, pp. 3-16.

18. See 15, p. 17.

19. See 6, pp. 927-928. One might claim that spokespersons for the poor or the rich have an obligation to competent analysts. But from whence would such an obligation spring? If it is based on a contract between the spokesperson and a client, whether rich or poor, the only obligation taken on by the analyst is to live up to the terms of the contract. If this piece of paper specifies "competence," well and good; the spokesperson then has an obligation to be "com-

petent.'' But if there is no explicit mention of this requirement, the analyst can have no such obligation.

The bishops, however, have no contract at all with "the poor.'' They are spokesmen for them only in the sense that their goal is to promote the economic interests of those with low incomes. Were they to have any obligation to the poor because of this, it would interfere with their constitutionally guaranteed rights of free speech. Under the laws of the land, anyone may climb up on a soapbox, and defend the interests of whatever group he wishes, without thereby taking on any "obligation" to defend them adequately. The alternative analysis would have a very dulling effect indeed on our exercise of free speech rights. (I owe this point to James Sadowsky.)

20. See 3, p. 32.

21. See 20.

22. Brown criticizes the Lawler argument on the ground that it "presupposes a falsely dualistic view of the world ..., radically sundering religion and daily life ..." (see 6, p. 927), and that therefore the bishops should be allowed, nay, encouraged, to speak out on economic affairs. Yet his collegiality, curiously enough, does not extend to the publication of the Lay Letter (see 25). In an unjustified and vituperative dismissal of that document, Brown calls it a "spectacle," urges us to "ignore" it, and casts aspersions on the theological expertise of its authors. This comes with particular ill-grace from a person who has severely criticized credentialism when applied to the bishops by their detractors.

23. See 24, p. 17.

24. See 28, p. 1. Says Michael Novak, "Is it right to divide the church along political lines? Should not the bishops stand above factions?''; 26, p. 32.

25. It may appear unseemly for a non-Catholic such as the present writer to presume to comment on the appropriateness of the U.S. bishops speaking out on economics. Protocol might indicate discreet silence as the best policy. But to succumb to this temptation would be to violate a canon of social science according to which truth or falsity is the criterion of judgment, and the person or antecedents of the analyst are strictly irrelevant. An interesting interchange on this matter goes as follows:

> Paul Heyne: I hope we can all agree that sociological criticisms of ideas are both useful and dangerous. They are useful because ideas do have causes. And they are dangerous because such criticisms too easily degenerate into ignoring the validity of the ideas and concentrating on *ad hominem* attacks and assumed motives. I think this applies to both sides in the general discussion in which we are engaged. It's easy for defenders of capitalism, such as myself, to ignore the clerical critics, such as Gregory Baum, by claiming that everything they say is a result of status anxiety. And it's easy for the clerical critics of capitalism to dismiss, or heavily discount, the arguments of economists who are, I think, the principal formulators of arguments to defend capitalism. It's much too

easy for them to dismiss these arguments on the grounds that, well, all social scientists operate in some kind of value framework.

Now, having said that it's both useful and dangerous, what follows from it? I think one thing, maybe, follows from it. *Sociological explanations should only be provided by people for those movements in which they, themselves, participate. Don't do it to your enemies. Do it to yourself* (emphasis added).

Milton Friedman: May I just interject that I think that's utterly wrong. I don't want to be in a position where I say, 'I only want a physician to advise me on cancer if he's had cancer.' I think sociologists ought to study whatever sociologists study.

Morality of the Market: Religious and Economic Perspectives, Walter Block, Geoffrey Brennan & Kenneth Elzinga, eds.; Vancouver: The Fraser Institute, 1985, pp. 387-88.
In a similar vein, James Schall, S.J., states:

(Consider) the propriety of criticizing Catholic popes and bishops for positions they take on economics or politics. It seems to me that one ought to ask oneself first, to what audience are we talking when we are talking about criticizing a pope or a bishop or even a lowly Jesuit. What is the audience? If it is the university audience, if it is an academic audience, the presupposition is intellectual; the presumption is one of integrity and freedom. And the Catholic church, it seems to me, historically, and indeed in practically any document in which this issue is discussed, has always taken the following position: that it is important and vital for people who disagree, whether they be within the church or Protestants, Jews, Muslims, whatever they may be, and this includes total non-believers, to state fairly and correctly and as bluntly as they wish what their problems are with the position of the Catholic Church, or with a given individual in the church.

To do this, in my view, is not in any sense to insult the dignity or the stature or the status of the person or the author to whom you are addressing yourself. Now it is obviously possible, even for a professor, to be unfair and snide and bitter. We know that happens. But in general, an honest man says, 'I have read the position of the Catholic Church and I have the following difficulties with it which to me are very serious.' Within the tradition of the Catholic Church, it seems to me, and within the tradition of the intellectual integrity of which they ought to be obliged, one should say, 'I appreciate very much the honor you do to us, to me, to state what you hold and why you hold it.' And in the context of academic freedom and intellectual integrity, one can respond to that. See James Schall, S.J., "Ethical Reflections on the Economic Crisis," in *Theology*, Third World Development and Economic Justice, Walter Block and Donald Shaw, eds., Vancouver: The Fraser Institute, 1985, pp. 83-84.

26. Actually, there is strong evidence which indicates that this document reflects not the views of the bishops, but those of their staffs. See in this regard Philip F. Lawler, *How Bishops Decide: An American Catholic Case Study*, Washington, D.C.: Ethics and Public Policy Center, 1986, especially pp. 24-34; also Dinesh D'Souza, "Whose Pawns Are the Bishops?" *Policy Review*, Fall 1985.

27. See 6, p. 928.

28. See 18, p. 49.

29. See 6, p. 928.

30. See 29, p. 5; 18, p. 49; 39, p. 13.

31. This view was ascribed to *Fortune* by the *New York Times*, which stated, "socialism gives them (the bishops) a role to play, while capitalism — reliance on imperfect market forces — leaves them out in the cold" (see 17, p. 17).

32. This novel hypothesis was put forth quite seriously in 38, p. 69. However, isn't it amazing that the American Enterprise Institute, the Heritage Foundation, the Ethics & Public Policy Centre, the Mises Institute, the Cato Institute and hundreds of other organizations have managed to maintain a semblance of support for the marketplace, despite their location in that den of socialist iniquity, Washington, D.C.?

33. See 17, p. 24.

34. See 7, p. 248.

35. See 11, p. 19.

36. See Gabriel Kolko, *The Triumph of Conservatism: A Reinterpretation of American History, 1900-1916*, Chicago: Quadrangle, 1963.

37. It shall be argued below that the bishops have failed to understand the injustice which exists in the economy, and while they have correctly identified some of the victims, i.e. the poor, they have misconstrued the reason for making this claim, and have failed to point out the real perpetrators: businessmen, working with sympathetic government officials.

38. See 16, p. 9.

39. See Frances Piven and Richard Cloward, *Regulating the Poor: The Functions of Public Welfare*, New York: Random House, 1971.

40. It would appear that Brown has failed to give sufficient weight to this distinction. See 5, p. 129, point 5.

41. See 25, p. 58.

42. See 36, p. 338.

43. This point was made by Walter Block, *Focus: On Economics and the Canadian Bishops*, Vancouver: The Fraser Institute, 1983, pp. 5-6, which is a critique of the pastoral letter on the economy "Ethical Reflections on the Economic Crisis," written by the Social Affairs Committee of the Canadian Conference of Catholic Bishops.

44. *Seattle Post-Intelligencer*, December 12, 1984, p. E-9. Cited by Paul Heyne, 15, p.19, fn. 10.

45. See 15, p. 11

46. The two, as we shall see below, are Michael Novak, author of numerous treatises on economics, and Paul Heyne, a professional economist, and author of a best-selling university textbook, *The Economic Way of Thinking* (SRA Press, Fourth Edition, 1983). This is not by a long shot the first time non-economists such as the bishops have eclipsed professional economists, but it certainly gives pause for thought to those who have rejected BP on grounds of credentialism.

47. See 19, p. 112.

48. Material in brackets supplied by present author; 24, p. 12; See also 19, p. 122.

49. Material in brackets supplied by present author; see 24, p. 8.

50. Material in brackets supplied by present author; see 24, p.8.

51. This book, New York: McGraw-Hill, 1982, comes especially to mind because Walter Williams is listed as one of those who have given testimony to the Lay Commission on Catholic Social Teaching and the U.S. economy, in its preparation of the Lay Letter. See 25, p.88.

52. It is beyond the scope of a footnote, however large, merely to list all the insightful critiques made by Novak in this regard. Such an enterprise would require a lengthy review essay. However, even a cursory mention of Novak's work would include the following: *The Spirit of Democratic Capitalism*, N.Y.: Simon & Shuster, 1982; *The Corporation : A Theological Inquiry*, Washington, D.C.: The American Enterprise Institute, 1981; *Capitalism and Socialism: A Theological Inquiry*, Michael Novak, ed., Washington, D.C.: The American Enterprise Institute, 1979; "A Theology of Development for Latin America" in *On Liberation Theology*, Ronald H. Nash, ed., Milford, Michigan: Mott, 1984.
    It is impossible to reconcile Novak's denial that the poor are subjugated by government economic intervention with this wealth of insightful material showing just the opposite.
    See also 25, p. 42, where Novak exposes the hypocrisy of businessmen who "complain about governmental regulations which they don't like (and) are the first to ask government for regulations which they do like."

53. See 15, pp. 3-4, 8. Material in brackets supplied by present author.

54. Says Heyne:

> The demand for the services of productive resources is like all other demand curves: it slopes downward to the right. Other things remaining equal, a larger quantity will be demanded at lower prices and a smaller quantity at higher prices. In the case of productive resources, this relationship may be so well disguised that people won't see it or will refuse to believe it. But the relationship will hold whether it's recognized or not.

The best example is probably the case of labor services demanded by an employer. Employers purchase labor services after estimating the probable contribution those services will make toward the creation of income. They hire when they expect the additional revenue from a hiring decision to be greater than the additional cost which that decision entails. They use the simple rule of Chapter 9: take those actions and only those actions whose expected marginal revenue is greater than their expected marginal cost. The higher the wage rate, the higher the marginal cost of purchasing labor services. Other things remaining equal, therefore, a smaller quantity of labor services will be demanded as the price that must be paid to obtain them goes up.

Why is this so widely and frequently denied? It's denied, for example, by those who insist that opposition to legal minimum wages is evidence of indifference toward the plight of the poor. But do poor people really benefit from legislated increases in the minimum wage? If the legal minimum is no higher than what employers are already paying, it has no effect. It will have an impact only if some covered employers are paying less than the legal minimum. But won't these employers lay some workers off if they're compelled to pay a higher wage, or at least not replace workers who quit?

'They wouldn't have to' isn't a good answer. It's a common answer, because so many people believe that employers pay wages 'out of profits' and can therefore refrain from laying workers off when wage rates rise, so long as profits are adequate to cover the increased wages. This seems to imply that the quantity of labor services demanded is a constant, dictated perhaps by technology, so that the only options before employers are either to pay the higher wage rates or to close down the operation. But the demand for labor services is not perfectly inelastic and will at times be highly elastic, because employers can almost always find substitutes, within some range, for labor services of a particular type.

The Economic Way Of Thinking, op.cit. pp. 229-230.

55. In contrast, the Austrian school of economics places purposive behaviour at centre stage of its analysis. See for example, Ludwig von Mises, *Human Action*, Chicago: Regney, 1966; Murray N. Rothbard, *Man, Economy & State*, Los Angeles: Nash, 1970.

56. Terry Anderson, P.J. Hill, *The Birth of a Transfer Society*, Stanford, California: Hoover Institution Press, 1980.

57. Ayn Rand has anticipated BP in this regard. See her *Atlas Shrugged*, New York: Random House, 1957.

58. See 19, pp. 112, 113.

59. To be fair to the Novak position, it must be remembered that in his view, capitalism is virtually completely impotent in the absence of its appropriate spiritual, cultural and political predispositions and antecedents.

60. This felicitous phrase was coined by Robert Nozick. See his *Anarchy, State & Utopia*, New York: Basic Books, 1984.

61. To use a phrase coined by the greatest free market rhetorician to have ever become President, Ronald Reagan.

62. See 39, p. 10; 7, p. 247.

63. See 19, p. 111.

64. See 5, p. 129.

65. See 36, p. 339; precedence on this, however, belongs to the Canadian Conference on Catholic Bishops. See Supra 42.

66. See 3, pp. 32, 33.

67. See *New York Times* editorial, as cited in 30, p. 2; also see 14, p. 36.

68. For the present author's views on the ethics of abortion, see "Woman and Fetus: Rights in Conflict?" *Reason*, Vol.9, No. 12, April 1978, pp 18-25.

69. Countries with less than 100 people per square mile — and less than $1,000 per capita income in 1981 — include Colombia, Algeria, Chile, Guyana, Bolivia, Liberia, Congo, Tanzania, Kenya, Afghanistan, Ethiopia. See Thomas Sowell, *The Economics and Politics of Race, op. cit.*, pp. 208-17.

BIBLIOGRAPHY

1. Cesar A. Arredondo, "Help the Poor Now: A Practical Plan," *Catholicism in Crisis*, Vol. 3, No. 3, February 1985, pp. 14-16.

2. Doug Bandow, "On Matters of Economics, the Pope Is All Too Fallible," *The Register*, October 12, 1984, p. 52.

3. Peter L. Berger, "Can the Bishops Help the Poor?," *Commentary*, February 1985, pp. 31-35.

4. Tom Bethell, "Hilton Spirituality," *The American Spectator*, January 1985, pp. 7-9.

5. Robert McAfee Brown, "Appreciating the Bishops' Letter," *The Christian Century*, Vol. 101, No. 5, February 6-13, 1985, pp. 129-130.

6. Robert McAfee Brown, "On Getting Ready for the Bishops' Pastoral Letter," *The Christian Century*, Vol. 101, No. 30, October 10, 1984, pp. 927-928.

7. Trudy Bloser Bush, "Challenging Consciences," *The Christian Century*, Vol. 102, No. 8, March 6, 1985, pp. 246-250.

8. *Business Week*, "The Church and Capitalism: A Report by Catholic Bishops on the U.S. Economy Will Cause a Furor," November 12, 1984, pp. 104-112.

9. *The Church Economic Programs Information Service Bulletin*, "Background — The Catholic Bishops' Economic Letter," pp. 3-4, undated.

10. John C. Dwyer, "Politics, Morality and the Economic Pastoral," *Catholicism in Crisis*, Vol. 3, No. 5, April 1985, pp. 19-23.

11. Frans Alting von Geusau, "Are the Bishops Squandering Their Authority?," *Catholicism in Crisis*, Vol. 3, No. 4, March 1985, pp. 17-19.

12. Michael Goldberg, "Two Letters on the Economy: Two Sides of the Same Coin?," *The Christian Century*, Vol. 102, No. 12, April 10, 1985, pp. 347-350.

13. Ari L. Goldman, "Bishops' Letter on Economy Gets 'New Lift,'" *The New York Times*, June 16, 1985, p. 19; Ari L. Goldman, "The Church and the Poor," *The New York Times*, June 17, 1985.

14. Andrew M. Greely, "A 'Radical' Dissent," *Challenge & Response*, Robert Royal, ed., Washington, D.C.: Ethics & Public Policy Center, 1985, pp. 33-47.

15. Paul Heyne, "The U.S. Catholic Bishops and the Pursuit of Justice," *Cato Policy Analysis*, No. 50, March 5, 1985.

16. James Hitchcock, "Two Views on the Economy: A Comparison of the Bishops' and Lay Commission's Letters," *Catholicism in Crisis*, Vol. 3, No. 3, February 1985, pp. 7-9.

17. Eugene Kennedy, "America's Activist Bishops," *The New York Times Magazine*, August 12, 1984, pp. 14-30.

18. Charles Krauthammer, "Perils of the Prophet Motive," *The New Republic*, December 24, 1984, reprinted in *Challenge & Response*, Robert Royal, ed., Washington, D.C.: Ethics and Public Policy Center, 1985, pp. 48-53.

19. John Langan, Brian Benested, Donald Warwick and Michael Novak, "Four Views of the Bishops' Pastoral, the Lay Letter, and the U.S. Economy," Walter Burns, ed., *This World*, Winter 1985, pp. 99-117.

20. Phillip F. Lawler, "At Issue Is the Prophet Motive," *Wall Street Journal*, November 13, 1984, p. 30.

21. Frank Meinen, "Thou Shalt Not Steal," *A Voice from the Pews*, Vol. I, No. 2, April 1985.

22. Michael Novak, "The Bishops and the Poor," *Commentary*, May 1985, pp. 20-22.

23. Michael Novak, "Blaming America: A comment on paragraphs 202-204 of the First Draft," *Catholicism in Crisis*, Vol. 3, No. 8, July 1985, pp. 12-16.

24. Michael Novak, "Toward Consensus: Suggestions for Revising the First Draft, Part I," *Catholicism in Crisis*, Vol. 3, No. 4, March 1985, pp. 7-16.

25. Michael Novak, et al., *Toward the Future: Catholic Social Thought and the U.S. Economy — A Lay Letter*, New York: Lay Commission on Catholic Social Teaching and the U.S. Economy, 1984.

26. Michael Novak, "The Two Catholic Letters on the U.S. Economy," *Challenge and Response*, Robert Royal, ed., Washington, D.C.: Ethics and Public Policy Center, 1985, pp. 30-32.

27. John J. O'Connor, "Catholic Social Teaching and the Limits of Authority," *Challenge & Response*, ed., Robert Royal, Washington, D.C.: Ethics & Public Policy Center, 1985, pp. 75-80.

28. Lawrence W. Reed, "God Is Not a Socialist," *Answers to Economic Problems*, Vol. 11, No. 1, January 1985, pp. 1-2.

29. *The Religion and Society Report*, "The Bishops and Economic Democracy," Vol. 2, No. 1, January 1985, pp. 5-6.

30. *The Religion and Society Report*, "Special Report on Catholic Bishops and American Economics," March 1985.

31. Enrique T. Rueda, "The Bishops' Tired Old Solution," *Chicago Tribune*, November 27, 1984, p. 11.

32. Robert J. Samuelson, "The Lessons of Europe," *Challenge & Response*, Robert Royal, ed., Washington, D.C.: Ethics & Public Policy Center, 1985, pp. 65-67.

33. Daniel Seligman, "Keeping Up," *Fortune*, December 24, 1984, p. 149.

34. Leonard Silk, "A Call for Economic Change Based on Moral View," *The New York Times*, November 12, 1984, p. B11.

35. Robert L. Spaeth, "Relying on Government," *Catholicism in Crisis*, Vol. 3, No. 3, February 1985, pp. 12-13.

36. U.S. Bishops' Pastoral Letter on Catholic Social Teaching and the U.S. Economy; *Origins*, NC Documentary Service, November 15, 1984, Vol. 14, No. 22/23.

37. *Wall Street Journal*, "Capitalism and the Bishops," November 13, 1984, p. 30.

38. George F. Will, "God's Liberal Agenda," *Challenge & Response*, Robert Royal, ed., Washington, D.C.: Ethics & Policy Center, 1985, pp. 68-70.

39. Christopher Wolfe, "We Must Transform Ourselves First," *Catholicism in Crisis*, Vol. 3, No. 3, February 1985, pp. 10-11.